# 200 YEARS *of* BRITAIN'S RAILWAYS

IN 14 JOURNEYS

For my mum, Minoo

# 200 YEARS *of* BRITAIN'S RAILWAYS

## IN 14 JOURNEYS

Sherin Aminossehe

FRANCES LINCOLN

NERO
NERO
NERO

# CONTENTS



*(front cover)*
*Britannia Bridge*
*(back cover)*
*Liverpool Lime Street facade*
*(opposite)*
*The grandeur of Liverpool Lime Street Station*

# FOREWORD

In 2025, we celebrate a really notable 200th anniversary – that of the first public passenger railway in the world.

The railway changed the world forever; part of the Industrial Revolution, it enabled urbanization, big industry, brought fresh food and milk to cities, and coal as fuel to every part of every nation. That seismic change started with the first journey on the Stockton & Darlington Railway in September 1825.

In the years that followed, the railway revolution took place. Building on the canal companies, the railways were the first modern businesses; they forced the harmonization of time across the country, and their construction and engineering changed the landscape of Britain.

As it was then, so it has been ever since. Despite gloomy prognostications, the railway is still very much part of twenty-first-century life. The British railway system has survived two world wars (and helped win them both), recessions, the rise of personal motoring, the Beeching cuts, and, more recently, Covid. Indeed, during the Covid lockdowns, for some of us, it was the recollection of great journeys by train to places we couldn't then go to, that kept us sane.

When Sherin asked me to write this foreword, my mind went back to Covid; stuck at home, in front of a screen or an iPhone, with little stimulation. It was a real joy when she started to do a series of drawings on Twitter for her friends, of the places they yearned to be visiting. In my case, she drew an evocative picture of a train on the Royal Albert Bridge, which connects Devon and Cornwall. For me, it's the most significant part of the journey from London to West Cornwall, the birthplace of my father, and a place we've had happy family holidays for all of my own seven decades. If it didn't make me cry, it certainly brought a tear to my eye; and thanks to her generosity, it now has a place in my study at home.

*(opposite) London Bridge Station*

So a much bigger sequel, of pictures of journeys by train around Great Britain, seems natural, specifically, of the stations and structures you can, or would have, encountered. View the grandeur of the huge Victorian stations of London and other major cities, the memorable points of departure and arrival of significant journeys; the lovely, smaller stations of the great railways, and some of the extraordinary bridges, viaducts and other constructions you would see or travel over.

As you turn these pages, if the images don't remind you of travels past, then they may stimulate you to travel in the future. By train, the journey is as good as the joy of arrival (or it should be!). The British have a love/hate relationship with the railway, which is as it should be, since, after all, we invented travel by train!

As Commissioner for Transport for London, I was surrounded by the work of my forebears, the giants of Ashfield and Pick; the roundel, the Johnston typeface, the architecture, the sense of good order and purpose; all of which – notwithstanding day-to-day perturbations – are apparent to even a casual traveller. I felt the responsibility of carrying on that tradition keenly. As Chair of Network Rail, with my brilliant Chief Executive, Andrew Haines (now, joyfully and deservedly, Sir Andrew), we were, (and he still is), the custodians of the whole of the infrastructure of the British railway network. Neither of us took it lightly; Sherin's evocative pictures are of buildings and structures that should be cherished and conserved for the future, and we have tried to do that, aided by the Railway Heritage Trust, which helps to find uses for fine, old, but redundant, railway buildings.

But maybe that might be to end on too serious a note. The truth is, the subjects of Sherin's drawings are all extraordinary testimony to the creators of our great railway heritage; but the real joy is that you would have to be terribly dull, or untravelled, not to have enjoyed travelling to and from them, or to have relished being where they are.

I really hope you enjoy every page of this lovely book, as I've done. We owe Sherin a debt of gratitude for her work to create this wonderful collection.

**Peter, Lord Hendy of Richmond Hill**
Minister of State for Rail
Department of Transport
January 2025

8-9

# INTRODUCTION

*Railway termini are our gates to the glorious and the unknown.*
*Through them we pass out into adventure and sunshine ...*
E. M. Forster (1879–1970)

I begin with a memory of a journey, starting with the edge of the glowing sky, underlined with a pink light, hinting at the day to come. The air is crisp with a chill breeze that brings with it the smell of the fried fat of the fast-food outlets. The tinny tannoy occasionally comes to life and drones in the background, while the reassuring clickety-clack of the indicator board announces departures and arrivals. I feel a small thrill: not a feeling most people would associate with modern-day Euston station, but I've always loved the railways.

I went to University College London and effectively grew up around Euston – its grey, granite-hard surfaces were weirdly welcoming, despite the wind tunnel effect of the open-air courtyard that made my A1 portfolio practically take off while my hands clutched at its handle, my five-foot frame struggling to stop it getting airborne. It felt an odd rite of passage.

But it hasn't just been Euston. When my parents and I arrived in the United Kingdom from Iran, our travel choices were somewhat limited, given the visa issues that came with a lack of British citizenship, so I have fond memories of railway trips in the eighties: of Torquay station with its austere Victorian turrets; Derby, which served as a gateway to Alton Towers; and the Snowdonia Mountain Railway, in North Wales, which, despite the unceasing fine mist of rain, charmed my parents with its mountain vistas and reminded them of northern Iran.

*Bristol Temple Meads Station*

Later, stations became a portal to spend weekends with friends, with trips to Leicester, Cambridge and Bristol (my first introduction to the beautiful Bristol Temple Meads). Later still, and when the professional world beckoned, I travelled extensively across the UK, mesmerized by the ticket hall in Hull Paragon Station, the roof of Edinburgh Waverley, the red sandstone in Nottingham and Manchester stations both past and present, the grand curve of York and the art-deco architecture of Cardiff Central, to name just a few.

Holidays also had a strong railway element. My then boyfriend (now husband), Terence has an even bigger love of rail travel than I do. We took trains in China in the nineties through stations that teemed with humanity, dotted with kiosks that sold life insurance, and went on a round-the-world holiday that introduced me to rail travel in the United States through the magnificent Grand Central Station in New York and Washington DC's Union Station. We also travelled across Canada and, closer to home, went across Germany to Austria, enjoying the beauty of many trips on Swiss mountain railways, with their leisurely pace and expansive vistas. Finally, nothing could quite beat the honeymoon he had planned which he still, tongue-in-cheek, calls 'the 10:40 departure from Platform 1 Victoria Station to

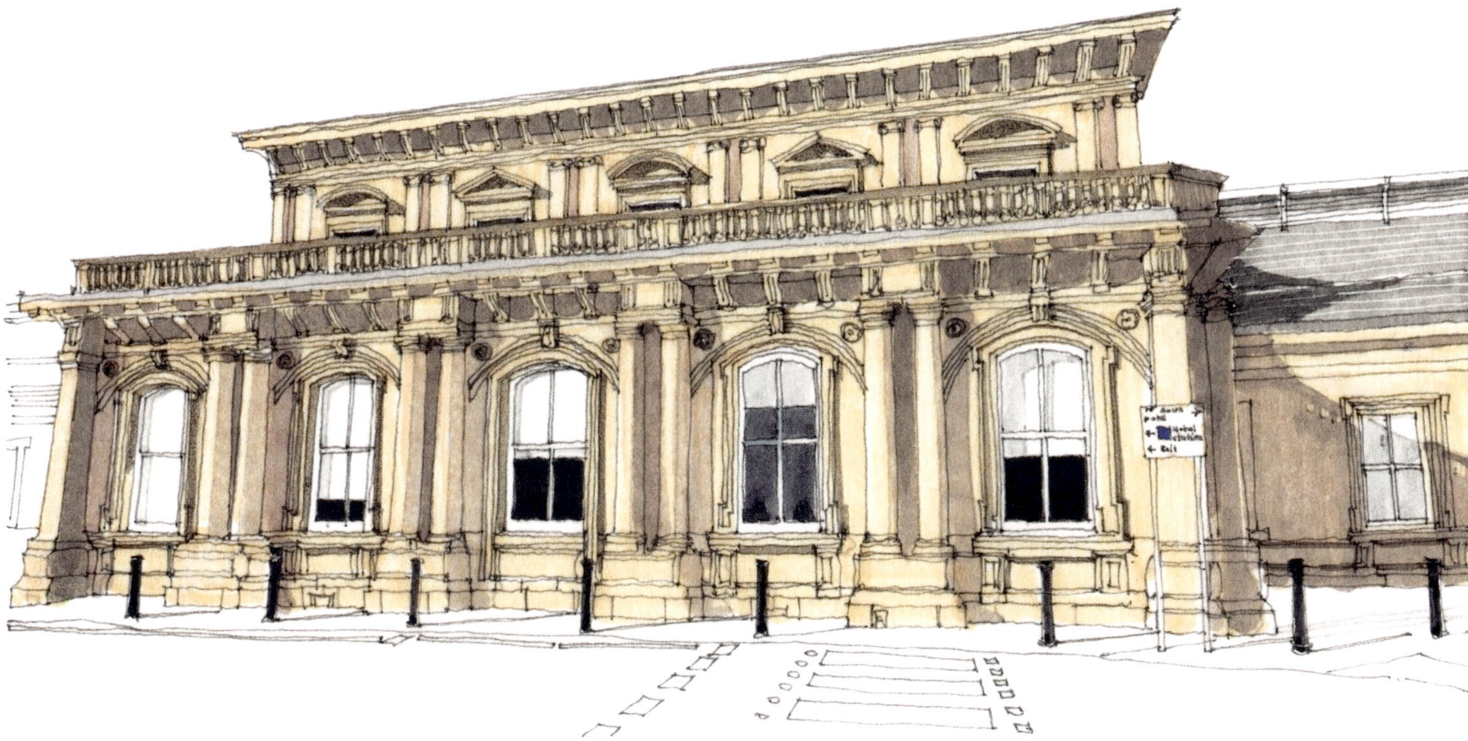

*The external facade of Hull Paragon Station*

Margate', which of course is the Orient Express, a service that propels Victoria Station into the glamorous early twentieth-century days of rail travel.

As E. M. Forster wrote, train stations have always been much more than interchanges or places to transit: the sensations, the promise of travel, the names of faraway places, the architecture – like a cathedral – they are a reminder of grander times; with small details and inscriptions that hide in plain sight, telling untold stories of the past while setting the scene for what will be the tales of the future.

As I write this, it's less than a year to the 200th anniversary of the first railway journey, when *Locomotion No. 1* went from Darlington to Stockton and effectively gave birth to the railway in the UK. As you go from journey to journey, chapter to chapter in this book, I will take you through some of these stations, starting in Darlington where it all began, and then travelling across the country.

This book is structured by journeys, taking in not just the architecture and detail of the stations, but also the people associated with them. We will also travel through time, discovering the lost stations on our routes, those that became economically unviable, fell out of fashion or were even demolished to make way for roads and urban expansion. We will also make slight detours to heritage lines.

Edinburgh Waverley ticket hall

Throughout this, we won't be forgetting the railway infrastructure: the signal boxes, bridges and viaducts without which our journeys wouldn't be possible.

A full-time job has meant it has not been possible to visit every single station and sit with a sketchbook to draw as I would have liked, so I have used photographs from many years of railway journeys (which shows that at the back of my mind this is a thing I had always wanted to do), as well as Network Rail's and Science Museum Group/National Railway Museum's extensive archives, to fill in the gaps. Talking of gaps, on a soggy spring day in May when I was due to speak at a conference in Leeds, I think I was the only commuter who saw the silver lining of our cancelled train, meaning that I had to go via another route (that took twice the time) and could cover a number of stations that I was keen to draw, including the station at Sheffield.

The book ends not just by looking through the past 200 years, but with cautious hope for the future as we end our final journey at Birmingham Curzon Street. A lost station standing derelict for many decades, which was once the terminus of the London (Euston) to Birmingham line and the world's first intercity railway, it will come back into use as part of HS2 and so bring us full circle.

*Manchester Victoria Station*

## NOTE ON THE DRAWINGS

For those of you with an artistic bent, all of the drawings here have been drawn with 0.05 and 0.03 fine liners to capture some of the remarkable architectural detail. The colour is truly mixed media, the materials used range from gouache and watercolour to Indian ink, brush pens, pastel and more oily coloured pencils, acrylic pens and even some Tippex for highlights!

LOCOMOTION

JOURNEY

I

# THE FIRST JOURNEY

## SHILDON *to* STOCKTON

SHILDON

HEIGHINGTON

DARLINGTON NORTH ROAD

ST JOHN'S CROSSING STOCKTON

The world changed forever on the morning of 27th September 1825. As dawn broke, *Locomotion No.1* passed through towns and over iron bridges and the first modern railway journey began, uniting towns and ushering in a new era. This first journey reshaped commerce, travel and communities and heralded the birth of modern railways and the promise of progress.

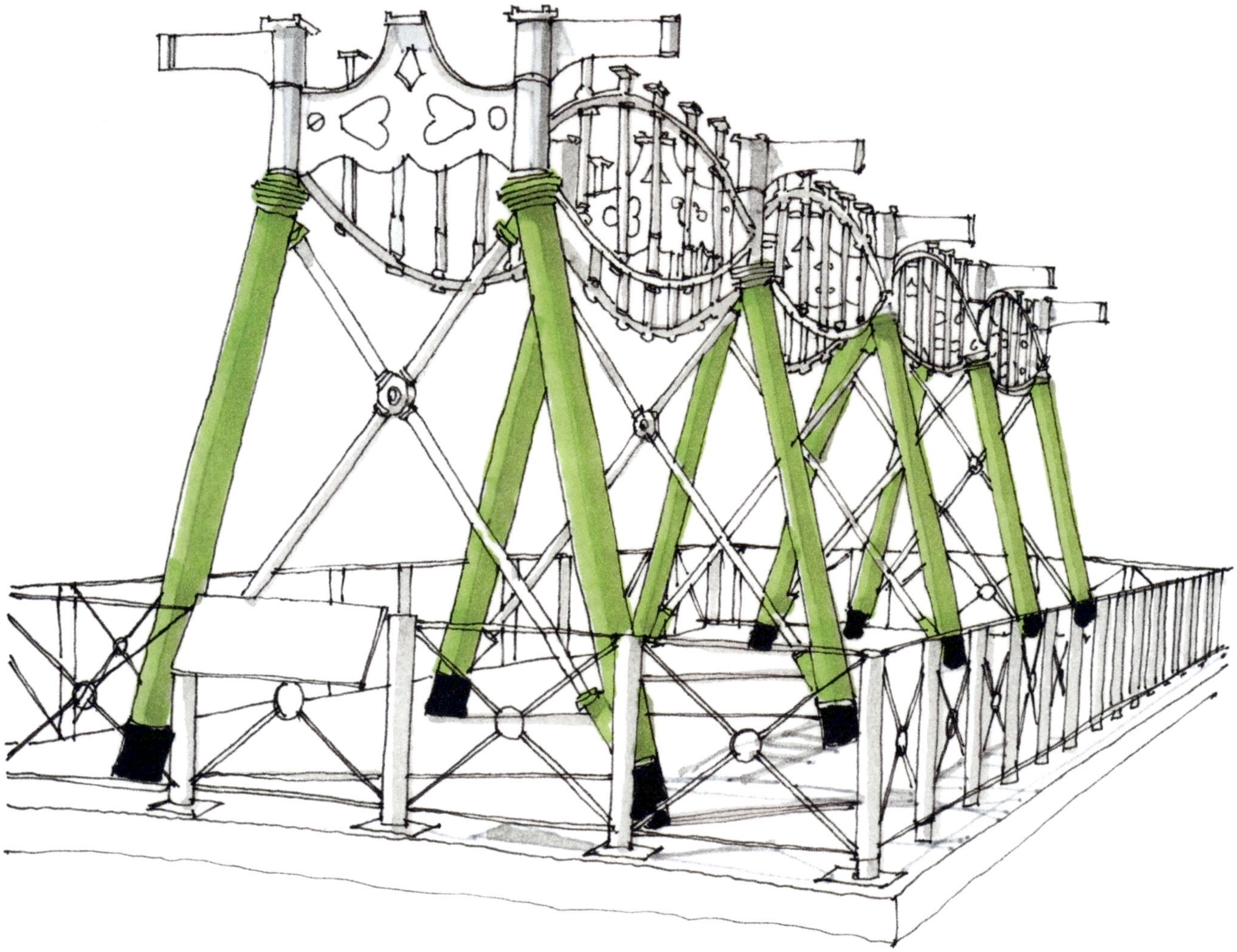

## THE JOURNEY

According to contemporary newspaper accounts, the day started very early at 5 a.m., when the passenger-carrying wagons were already fully occupied. At this stage – and ironically for the first railway journey – they were drawn by horses along the railway from Darlington towards the 'permanent steam engine' just below Brusselton Tower, as the first 13km (8 miles) from the colliery were too steep for the locomotives of the day. Cottages and the engine reservoir – used to create steam to power the stationery engine – can still be seen at the Brusselton Incline.

*Locomotion No. 1*, George Stephenson's engine, was waiting for them at Mason's Arms level crossing in Shildon, where over 500 passengers embarked. The engine and the wagons had been brought from Wilton Colliery across the Gaunless Bridge. Built by Stephenson in 1823, this was an early iron bridge, the very first to use an iron truss and the first lenticular truss bridge, meaning the top and bottom of the truss each had an arch that formed a lens shape. The bridge was manufactured by John & Isaac Burrell, but the year after its construction, heavy snow led to flooding that damaged it. The bridge was then rebuilt to four-span form in 1825, in time for *Locomotion No. 1*'s maiden voyage. Unfortunately, by 1901, the bridge's structure could no longer cope with the weight of the coal wagons and it had to be replaced. The stone base of the bridge across the River Gaunless can still be seen, while its ironwork has been restored and resides at the museum in Shildon.

*(top) The Gaunless Bridge*
*(opposite) The original Heighington Station*

Continuing on with our 200-year-old journey, the article in the *Morning Post* goes on to describe how, 'the beasts of the field and the fowls of the air seem to view with wonder and awe the machine which now moved onward at the rate of 10 or 12 miles an hour [16 to 19 km/h]', making its way to Heighington, Darlington North Road at midday, and then finally to St John's Crossing in Stockton-on-Tees at around 3 p.m, where a massive crowd of 40–50,000 people had gathered. The celebratory dinner was also in keeping with the reception. The *Morning Post* described it as elegant and proceeded to detail the twenty-three toasts that were given, two of which were for the Liverpool & Manchester and the Leeds & Hull Railways (Journey 2). The last toast was, quite rightly, to George Stephenson but, exhausted by the events of the day, he had already retired.

### HEIGHINGTON

The buildings that we see at the site today were actually built in 1827, two years after the maiden voyage, with some railway cottages completed as accommodation three years later. They were in effect a proto-railway station – this was before the model of the railway station that we use today had developed – and they were built in the form of a public house. Listed at Grade II*, not surprising as it is effectively the world's first railway station, the buildings act as a marker for where *Locomotion No.1* was first placed on the rails in 1825, and where its boiler exploded in 1828.

### DARLINGTON NORTH ROAD

Darlington North Road Station's building is now a museum entitled Hopetown. It is dedicated to Darlington's role in the evolution of the railways and to the stories of the people who

BUS
STOP

*The current Darlington Station*

made it happen. It also houses *Locomotion No.1*. Opened in 1842 (and now listed as Grade II*), it was constructed to a design by the Stockton & Darlington engineer, John Harris (1812–69), was expanded and rebuilt on several subsequent occasions and was also one of the sites of the jubilee celebration for the 1825 voyage.

The current main Darlington Station is an important stop for a number of rail services, including London North Eastern Railway, Cross Country, Northern and the TransPennine Express. The building, dating from 1887, is a Grade II* structure and won the Large Station of the Year award in 2005. The station's designers were T. E. Harrison, chief engineer of North Eastern Railway – it opened just before his death in 1888 – and William Bell, their architect. Darlington is a beautiful example of a Victorian station with its detailed and elaborate ironwork and broad island

*'The proprietors of the above concern hereby give notice that the main line of railway commencing at Witton Park Colliery in the west of this county and terminating at Stockton-upon-Tees on the east, with the several branches to Darlington, Yarm etc, being about 27 miles in extent will be formally opened for the general purposes of trade on Tuesday the 27th Inst ... proceed at 9 o'clock precisely by way of Darlington and Yarm to Stockton-upon-Tees, where it is calculated they will arrive about 1 o'clock. An elegant dinner will be provided for the company who may attend ... A superior locomotive travelling engine, on the most improved construction will be employed, with a train of convenient carriages for the conveyance of the proprietors and strangers...'*

Stockton & Darlington Company's Office, 14 September 1825
(Manchester Guardian, 24 September 1825)

*Darlington North Road Station Museum*

**GEORGE STEPHENSON & ROBERT STEPHENSON**
(1781–1848 & 1803–59)

Two hundred years ago, on 27 September 1825, a short 40-km (25-mile) journey in the north-east of England transformed travel across the globe. Distances became shorter, communities became closer and railways helped business, towns and cities to thrive. The Stockton & Darlington Railway was the venue for the first modern railway journey and is the foundation of the next thirteen journeys in this book. It made possible the railways that were to follow, such as the Liverpool & Manchester Railway in the next journey. There are many in this story who have played important parts in the development of the railways, but arguably the man who deserves the title 'Father of the Railways', was George Stephenson. Together with his son, he was responsible for the first train journey with goods and passengers, railway lines and bridges, and undoubtedly laid the foundations for the railway system have today.

George Stephenson came from a humble background and had no formal education until eighteen, when he paid for his own lessons and showed his strong ability in mechanics. He had a range of jobs until eventually coming to work at Killingworth Colliery. There he impressed his employers with his ability and spent the next ten years honing his skills and building his first steam locomotive, a forerunner of *Locomotion No. 1*. Stephenson's growing interest can be seen from a letter dated 10 November 1822, during his time at Killingworth Colliery, which talks about his ideas regarding locomotive design.

In 1821, the same year that the Stockton & Darlington Railway Act passed through Parliament (a substantial piece of deal-making given the number of landowners involved), George Stephenson met Edward Pease. Pease, Stockton & Darlington's main shareholder

and promoter, is often referred to as 'Father of the Railways', and in what is now regarded as a seminal moment, Stephenson convinced Pease to use a steam locomotive to draw the train carriages instead of horses. Stephenson and his son, Robert, not only set up the company to construct the railway, but also, alongside Pease, set up another in Newcastle-upon-Tyne to build the railway engines for the Stockton & Darlington Railway, the first company in the world formed to do so. They also established the first standard gauge for railways – 143.5 cm (4ft 8½ in) – the same width that is still used not just in Britain, but in most railways throughout the world (Journey 5).

In 1825, the first locomotive for the railway was built. Now known as *Locomotion No. 1,* it was originally named *Active*, and was followed by *Hope*, *Diligence* and *Black Diamond*. The Stockton & Darlington Railway opened on 27 September 1825, with and engine driven by Stephenson. This chapter is their story.

The achievements of father and son did not end here. George Stephenson had a significant part in the Liverpool & Manchester Railway and his engine, *Rocket*, won the Rainhill Trials – held to determine whether locomotives or static engines should operate the new railway – in October 1829. As a result, he both built the engines for the Liverpool & Manchester Railway as well as being involved in the design of some of the stations, including Manchester Victoria (Journey 2). From 1830 onwards, he was much in demand, and the Father of the Railways even worked with the 'Railway King', George Hudson (Journey 11) and was chairman of the Yarmouth to Norwich line (Journey 4).

His son continued to work with him, including on the Norwich line. Robert was involved in the early design of Euston Station, where he is celebrated with a statue (Journeys 7 & 8) and also left behind some impressive railway bridges, including the Goole Swing Bridge (Journey 2), the High Level Bridge at Newcastle-upon-Tyne (Journey 11) and the tubular Britannia Bridge (Journey 7).

platforms. It also has an impressive tower with a station clock that apparently was not to the liking of the North Eastern Railway chairman, who complained too much money had been spent on it. In fact, you can clearly see where the money went and the influence of York and Newcastle Central Station on the wrought-iron structure of Darlington's roof and cast-iron columns. If you look up, you can also see North Eastern's coat of arms as well those of Darlington, Durham and Newcastle in alternate roof supports above the columns.

### ST JOHN'S CROSSING STOCKTON

The original building from 1825 still survives amongst an anonymous streetscape in Stockton-on-Tees. From the outside it is a very modest-looking structure; in some ways like the station at Headington, except that it is made of brick, it could almost be somebody's house. Today, it is used as a homeless shelter. The only things that give you a hint of the importance of the Grade II listed buildings are two tablets affixed to its walls.

The first says: 'The first rail of the Stockton & Darlington Railway was laid on the adjacent level crossing in May 1822'. The other reads: 'Here in 1825 Stockton and Darlington Railway Company booked the first passenger thus making an epoch in the history of mankind'.

*(above) Stockton St John's Crossing Station*

*(opposite) Steam Locomotive Stockton and Darlington Railway No. 1 0-4-0 'Locomotion'*

## LOCOMOTION NO.1

This part of the book is not a lengthy analysis of bogies, air brakes and breakdown valves. However, *Locomotion No. 1*, or, to give it its full name, *Steam Locomotive Stockton and Darlington Railway No. 1 0-4-0 'Locomotion'*, is different. It was the first steam-powered railway engine to run on a public railway and is now housed at the National Railway Museum in Shildon, County Durham. However, the engine will return to Darlington for an extended visit, in time for the bicentenary celebrations.

*Locomotion No. 1* was built by George and Robert Stephenson and their company Robert Stephenson and Co., and was ordered for the Stockton & Darlington Railway in 1824. It had a number of unique design features for the time, such as the coupling rods that linked the axles, which prevented the driving wheels from slipping on the rails.

There are many models of *Locomotion No. 1*. There is a particularly special one that shows it going over the Gaunless Bridge. It is incredibly delicate and detailed, almost making you think that given the right kind of fuel the engine could travel across the Gaunless River once more.

HUDDERSFIELD & MANCHESTER RAILWAY & CANAL COMPANY
INCORPORATED 1845
DEVANT SI JE PUIS

JOURNEY

# 2

# THE TRANSPENNINE

## HULL *to* LIVERPOOL

HULL PARAGON STATION

GOOLE SWING BRIDGE

LEEDS

HUDDERSFIELD

MANCHESTER VICTORIA

MANCHESTER CENTRAL STATION (LOST STATION)

MANCHESTER PICCADILLY

LIVERPOOL LIME STREET

LIVERPOOL CENTRAL STATION (LOST STATION)

This Journey along the TransPennine route reveals a narrative of railway heritage and resilience. Beginning at Hull Paragon, framed by Philip Larkin's literary echoes, the route flows through landmarks like the Goole Swing Bridge, Huddersfield's classical stately home grandeur and the historic vibrance of Manchester Victoria. Culminating in the architectural triumph of Liverpool Lime Street, this chapter tells the stories of migration and industrial heritage weaving together communities, cultures and narratives across the Pennines and beyond.

*'The departure of a vessel with emigrants from a foreign port is signalled to Hull by telegraph, together with the number of emigrants she carries. Preparations are then made by the emigration agent with the North-Eastern Railway Company, for trains to convey them to Liverpool... Sunday is the time of arrival; on Monday morning they disembark, and their luggage is examined by the Customs officials, after which they are taken to a large shed, specially fitted up for their convenience, situated on the South side of the Albert Dock. Breakfast is provided for them, after which the train is drawn up on a special siding, and they depart for Liverpool.'*

*Hull Daily News*, 10 October 1896

**PHILIP LARKIN**
(1929–85)

Larkin, considered to be one of Britain's best post-war poets, was born in Coventry and spent many decades of his adult life in Hull. He wrote a considerable number of his celebrated works in this city, chiefly in his role as university librarian at the Brynmor Jones Library at the University of Hull, a post he held until his death. Larkin is commemorated in Hull Paragon Station with a statue by sculptor Martin Jennings.

Amongst his writings are a number of poems about travel and train journeys, including 'Travellers' (published 2012) and 'Here' (1961). 'I remember, I remember' (1954) is about a journey through his home town of Coventry (more about that in Journey 7). But the best known is 'The Whitsun Weddings' (1958), which is based on a journey Larkin took in 1955, leaving Paragon Station and travelling to London King's Cross. It is atmospheric and descriptive; a bit like a summer dream full of the sensations and sounds of rail travel. The poems are all evocative of the sensation of travel, with fleeting landscapes and memories that move past and alienated fellow travellers.

All of this is very pertinent for the particular journey that follows, which took more than two million people from Hull to Liverpool en route to America between 1830 and the early twentieth century.

*The external facade of Hull Paragon Station*

*Hull Paragon Station ticket office*

### HULL PARAGON STATION

The statue of Philip Larkin by sculptor Martin Jennings (b.1957), unveiled in 2010 to mark the 25th anniversary of the poet's death, greets you as you enter Hull Paragon Station. It is a fitting tribute to celebrate a poet who called Hull home and used this station frequently. It is also a stop on the Larkin trail, which starts in the former station hotel next door, goes through Paragon and winds its way through the city. The statue's sculptor, Martin Jennings, is also known for his depiction of other writers and poets, notably Sir John Betjeman (1906–84) in St Pancras Station.

Larkin's statue wasn't there when I first experienced Paragon Station in the late nineties. As an architecture student, I was particularly captivated by the neo-classical Italianate facade and wonderful tiled walls and mosaic floor in the ticket hall. The walls are still all decked out in cream, green and brown Burmantofts tiling, surrounding the oak-panelled former ticket office. The booking hall tiling was carried out by Julius Whitehead & Sons of Leeds, and the terrazzo mosaic floor, with its North Eastern Railway motif, is by Hodkin & Jones Ltd of Sheffield, which, to this day still produces architectural plaster covings and cornices.

The building itself was designed by G. T. Andrews (1804–55), a rather colourful character whose interesting business dealings forced him to auction his art collection only four years after Paragon opened in 1847. The station was further extended by North Eastern Railway chief architect William Bell (1844–1919) between 1903–04. It is now listed Grade II*.

Many emigrants, mainly from Scandinavia, who travelled along our route from Hull to Liverpool would have gone through here. Right next door is the Grade II listed former immigrant station and railway platform where they would have arrived, segregated from the other passengers (mainly

*Hull Paragon Station interior, with statue of Larkin in the distance*

for health reasons). This complex dates from 1871 and was then extended again ten years later by Thomas Prosser (1817–88). The days of sea passages to America, though, are long past and today the building has been converted to a bar.

### GOOLE SWING BRIDGE

To travel to Doncaster (and ultimately Leeds), trains would have needed to cross the River Ouse. The Goole Swing Bridge opened in 1869, and was designed by Thomas Elliot Harrison (1808–88) for the North Eastern Railway. Originally a Londoner, born in Fulham, he was steeped in the railways through his father and he was also a friend of Robert Stephenson. He completed his apprenticeship five years after *Locomotion No. 1* went from Stockton to Darlington (Journey 1) and eventually became the chief engineer to the NER, where he stayed for the rest of his life. He also designed the Hull to Doncaster line, the Victoria Viaduct over the River Wear and collaborated with Stephenson on the High Level Bridge in Newcastle (Journey 11).

The bridge itself is one the oldest swing bridges still in operation and, when built, the second longest as well. It is also Grade II* listed, still operating on a lot of the original hydraulic machinery designed by Sir G. W. Armstrong (1810–1900), a well-known engineer, philanthropist and innovator. He also collaborated with the architect Robert Norman Shaw to build his home Cragside, the first to be lit by hydroelectricity.

### LEEDS

The TransPennine Express can take less than an hour to get to Leeds from Hull, stopping in Brough and Selby en route. The railways arrived for the first time in Leeds in 1834, initially to a station in Marsh Lane and then twelve years later to Wellington Station in Wellington Street.

HOTEL

*Leeds Station's art deco North Concourse*

A second station was opened in 1854 and named Leeds Central, although today's station is a consolidation of the two, which occurred in 1869. The building itself is a reconstruction, as the original buildings were badly bombed in the Second World War, with further change in 1967.

The most special part of Leeds Station is the art deco North Concourse designed by William Henry Hamlyn (1889–1968), architect of a number of other fine art deco buildings such as Euston House, Queens Hotel in Leeds and Becontree Station. It is very reminiscent of the ticket hall of Cardiff Central Station (Journey 6), particularly in its volume, use of skylights and wonderful bronze lamps that hang down, so it is surprising – and possibly horrific – to think that in the seventies this magnificent space was used partially as a car park! Fortunately, common sense (and some would say decency) prevailed in the late nineties, and it was restored to its former glory by Carey Jones architects.

**HUDDERSFIELD**

Huddersfield is only a short trip of 20 minutes from Leeds, but its architectural style couldn't be more different. 'A stately home with trains in it' was the way the BBC2 series *Town* described the Palladian, Corinthian-columned grandeur of Huddersfield Station. Its elevation is definitely more reminiscent of a set for *Brideshead Revisited* or a Jane Austen novel adaptation, with Mr Darcy standing in front of it instead of the statue of Harold Wilson – it could possibly even double as one of the many *Bridgerton* settings. In fact, going one step further, Huddersfield has the accolade of being one of only six mainline railway stations that is Grade I listed. The others are Paddington (Journeys 5 & 6), King's Cross (Journey 14), Bristol Temple Meads (Journey 6), Newcastle (Journey 11) and St Pancras (Journey 11).

Designed by the architect James Pigott Pritchett (1789–1868) and built by the firm of Joseph Kaye between 1846–50,

*(opposite) The Palladian frontage of Huddersfield Station*

*(above) Huddersfield Station roundels*

it was also a favourite of the architecture writer Nicholas Pevsner, who regarded it as one of the best early stations. It also boasts of two pubs within the classical station frontage, to either side of the main entrance: The Head Of Steam and The King's Head. Each pub has elaborate scrolled consoles and two armorial badges above each parapet, which are inscribed 'Huddersfield and Manchester Railway and Canal Company', at the north end, and 'Lancashire and Yorkshire Railway Company' at the south end. The Latin motto at the north end – 'Devant si je puis' (Forward if I am able) – is a rather curious one for a train company. One can only assume that in the days before PR gurus the significance of the conditional tone was noted.

The station was the first building to be constructed in a programme of works for St George's Square, owned by local MP and landowner Sir John Ramsden, and its grandeur is the result of its being built at the joint expense of the Huddersfield and Manchester Railway and Canal Company and the Manchester & Leeds Railway as well with strong encouragement of the land-owning Ramsdens. The foundation stone was laid by Josh Fitzwilliam, the Lord Lieutenant, on 9 October 1846, when a public holiday was declared and, apparently, church bells were rung from dawn till dusk. Once the station was built, the first statue that graced its frontage was of Sir Robert Peel in 1873; it was only in 1999 that the statue of Harold Wilson came to its present position, owing to the Sicilian marble that Peel had been sculpted from having crumbled away, leading to the statue being removed in 1949. The true celebrity though in Huddersfield Station is not an erstwhile politician, but a furry feline named Felix and his younger partner in crime, Bolt. The pair raised more than £240,000 for charitable causes with a Facebook page that had more than 24 million views annually. Sadly, Felix died in 2023, but Bolt continues

*Manchester Victoria Station*

to keep the station safe from unwanted pests and while welcoming fans from across the world.

The interior is not quite as imposing as the grand neo-classical facade and the beautifully designed and pedestrianized public realm at the front, though a number of original features remain such as the tiled art-deco ticket kiosk with its bronze mullions and case racks, and the platforms that are covered by two-wrought iron trusses, one very wide, both with elaborate bosses. Delving further into the English Heritage listing, we can also find the buffet and waiting room between Platforms 4 and 8 with their 'separate match-boarded structure with panelled pilasters, each taking paired brackets and cornice'.

This station makes the traveller want to linger, but it is time to go on to our next stop in our TransPennine journey, Manchester.

## MANCHESTER VICTORIA

Thirty minutes later and the journey to Manchester Victoria takes us back to the migration route from Hull.

Despite being significantly altered in the early part of the last century and also bombed during the Second World War, substantial parts remain of the original station by John Brogden (1798–1869) and George Stephenson, father of our railway infrastructure and at the time chief engineer of the Liverpool & Manchester Railway. This includes some of the original Italianate facade.

The listed 1909 extension is by William Dawes (1840–97). Not many architects can claim to be accredited with the design of a building more than ten years after their death. Some of the station's most special features are a number of art-nouveau-style glazed tiles and a beautiful stained-glass rotunda over the station café, a smaller version of the one that graces the Edinburgh Waverley ticket hall (Journey 10), all of which have been lovingly restored by the architecture firm BDP as part of the expansion of the original station in 2014. It also boasts one of the largest tiled maps of the rail networks, a more enduring way of checking routes than the paper copies we are used to today. However, one particularly sad loss is the overhead mini railway to carry parcels around the station, which stood between 1895–1940, until it was damaged during the Second World War.

Manchester Victoria was used by two of the main railway companies of the time, the Leeds Railway Company and the

Liverpool & Manchester Railway Company, whose route we are partly following on this journey to Liverpool Lime Street. The Liverpool & Manchester was also the world's first inter-urban steam-powered railway, an important part of what shaped the Industrial Revolution. Before it was constructed, The *Observer* newspaper quipped that it was faster for goods to go between New York and Liverpool than it was for them to go from Liverpool to Manchester. Fittingly, its Manchester terminus at Liverpool Road is now home to the Science and Industry Museum.

## MANCHESTER CENTRAL STATION (LOST STATION)

Manchester Central was on a different line to Victoria, the intriguingly named Cheshire Lines Committee (CLC), and would have required a slight detour to get there; now it is the home of a conference centre, formerly named the G-Mex, and now with its name restored to Manchester Central in honour of the original railway station.

The CLC was at one time the second largest railway in Britain and one of the predecessors that it absorbed was the Liverpool & Garston Railway through the Liverpool Central Station Railway Act. It would probably take another whole book to describe the history and evolution of the different railway lines and companies in north-west England, but one of the purposes of the CLC was to create a better and more direct route to Liverpool, with its route linking Manchester Central and Liverpool Central Stations intended to provide a closer terminus for those migrating to America.

The station itself was opened in 1880 and designed by the architect and civil engineer Sir John Fowler (1817–98), who was also responsible for the Forth Railway Bridge, and for employing the cut-and-cover method for London's Metropolitan Railway. It is also very much a survivor, probably ultimately saved by its Grade II* listing in 1963. There is a beautiful, atmospheric oil sketch of it by Adolphe Valette (1876–1942), an artist who painted a number of scenes in and around Manchester, at the Manchester Art Gallery (acquired quite recently in 2010), which shows how the station would have felt in its heyday when it had the recently completed Midland Hotel next door. While the station is no longer in operation today, at least those attending conferences can admire the majestic 64-m (210-ft) single-span roof with its wrought-iron truss structure.

*The old Manchester Central Station*

CENTRAL
STATION

Keep Left

*View on to the train platforms at Manchester Piccadilly Station*

## MANCHESTER PICCADILLY

I have admired this station's Grade II listed Victorian roof on many occasions. There is a Philip Larkin letter written to Monica Jones – found while I was researching this journey – in which he relates taking this route to Liverpool and then Belfast for a teaching job. I cannot be certain which Manchester station he passed through, but he writes, 'My train dashed through the weeping quarries of Derbyshire to the most dusk-ridden ruinous vision of Manchester imaginable'. I like to think that if he saw it now, he would be more charitable.

Originally named Store Street when it opened in 1842 and then rapidly renamed London Road five years later, it did not gain its current name until 1960. The concourse, with its 200-m- (650-ft-) long iron and glass train shed, dates to 1866 with further expansions in the 1880s. Unfortunately, time, multiple architects and engineers mean that it can be difficult to completely attribute the design and the Historic England listing for the structure summarizes this as '. . . some discrepancy over the attribution of the engineers responsible for the train shed's two phases with some sources suggesting the 1860s spans were designed by William Baker and the 1880s spans by Lewis Henry Moorsom (1835–1914). However, R. and J. Rankin have also been suggested as responsible for the earlier phase and the original drawings for the later spans are signed by William Baker.'

The 1960s redevelopment of the station probably looks much finer and optimistic in the posters drawn by Claude Buckle (1905–73) – a prolific artist who also created many railway posters held in the archives of the Science Museum group – than it does on a grey day.

## LIVERPOOL LIME STREET

A further hour takes us to our penultimate stop. A terminus station, opened in 1836, it has the accolade of being the oldest still-operating grand terminus mainline station in the world, and was designed by John Cunningham, Arthur Holme and John Foster Jr. It has been expanded numerous times during its life, the latest being the reopening of the North Western railway hotel next door in 2022, which was originally designed by Alfred Waterhouse and built in 1871.

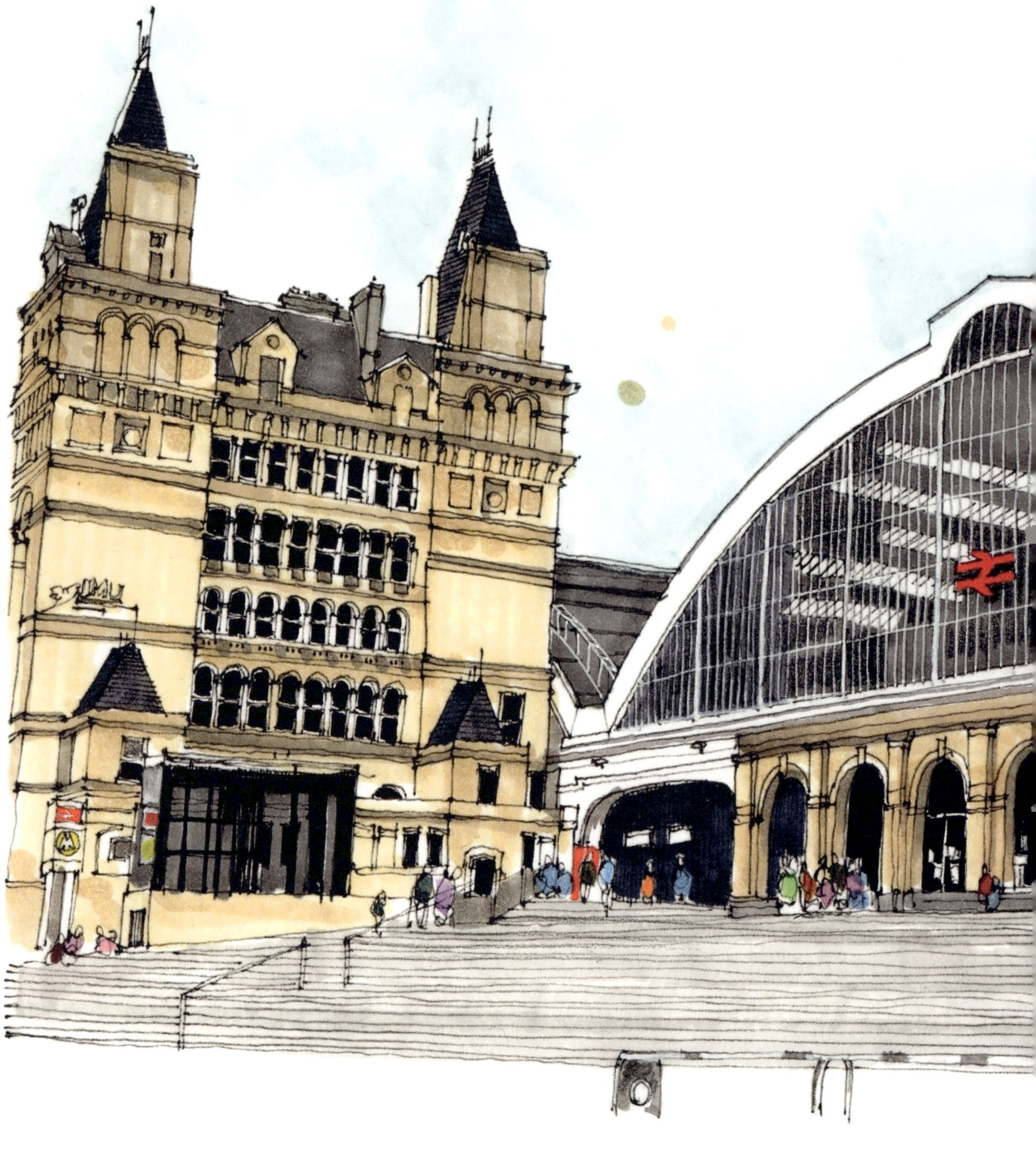
LJMU

*Liverpool Lime Street Station*

Aside from the streaming light coming from the uplifting canopy, the station boasts a number of unique features from its 'Tuscan columns', the sculpture of Ken Dodd and Bressie Braddock, to the wonderful electric synchronous clock made and installed by J. B. Joyce & Co (one of two major clockmakers that created station clocks – more in Journey 7). My own personal favourite though is the recently rediscovered plaque to Frank Hornby, the inventor of Meccano and the Hornby model railway, who was born on the site of the current station.

## LIVERPOOL CENTRAL STATION (LOST STATION)

Liverpool Central is now essentially an underground station opened in 1977 and is a central hub for Merseyrail, the original high-level station having been demolished in the seventies. Designed by Sir John Fowler in 1872, the main building fronted a single-arched train shed with a span of approximately 55m (180ft) that reached over 20m (65ft) at its highest point, quite similar to the design of Manchester Central.

Liverpool Central Station was at the western end of the CLC network, and it became the headquarters of the company and its Liverpool passenger terminus. The station didn't just offer journeys to and from Hull, but also to Stockport, Harwich, St Pancras and even Marylebone. It is interesting to note that the journey between Manchester Central and Liverpool Central then took 45 minutes compared to today's journey from Manchester Piccadilly to Lime Street, which is a little longer at 52 minutes.

Our emigrants' journey would have ended at this lost station, which would have been a busy, bustling space. The station apparently needed numerous porters and carters to move the possessions from the station to the docks, as well extra railway police officers, since migrants made an easy target for thieves and con artists. Their tickets would usually include a steamship ticket to Hull, the train ticket to Liverpool and finally a second steamship ticket to their ultimate destination, which was mainly America. Sometimes, so many emigrants arrived at one time that there would be up to seventeen carriages being pulled by one steam engine, a far cry from today's suburban, underground carriages.

*The old Liverpool Central Station*

BRITISH RAILWAYS
LIVERPOOL CENTRAL
WILLIAM ASHTON
Bargain Travel

FENCHURCH STREET STATION

JOURNEY

# 3

# EAST-END HOLIDAY

## FENCHURCH STREET *to* SOUTHEND

FENCHURCH STREET STATION

TILBURY RIVERSIDE &
TILBURY DOCK CRUISE TERMINAL

SOUTHEND VICTORIA

SOUTHEND CLIFF RAILWAY

SOUTHEND PIER RAILWAY

Beginning at London's Fenchurch Street Station, in an area steeped in history going back to Roman times, we travel to Tilbury Riverside, a neo-Georgian gem linked to the iconic *HMT Empire Windrush* and then over to Southend Victoria, with its nostalgic charm shaped by the railway's rise. Here we will discover the Edwardian innovation of Southend Cliff Railway and conclude at Southend Pier, riding trains along Britain's longest pier.

*Facade, Fenchurch Street Station*

**FENCHURCH**

Who better to show the enduring impact of railways on popular culture than Fenchurch, a literary character featuring in the bestselling series *The Hitchhiker's Guide to the Galaxy* by Douglas Adams, named because she was conceived in the ticket queue of the first station in our journey?

She is not an author, poet, architect, engineer or nineteenth-century industrialist, many of whom appear in these chapters, but is musical, and has a pair of speakers that 'would have impressed the guys who put up Stonehenge'. She appears in multiple forms throughout the five-book cycle.

Fenchurch is there from the first book's very first page, appearing as an unnamed woman sitting in the café in Rickmansworth, where she has a brilliant idea for making the world a better place before Earth is obliterated, and is at the end in *So Long and Thanks for All the Fish,* where she is now Arthur Dent's soulmate.

*'Fenchurch Street station is at the best of times a cheerless place. But yesterday it was wrapped in the remnants of a real London fog, which made it more cheerless than usual, yet it was with the difficulty that Inspector Izzard kept a clear space from the stairs to the platform. ... It was a little after 10, when the strains of the Guards' band heralded the Lancers approach, and as they made their way through the crowd, there were cheers, which almost lifted the mood, many rushing forward to pack the troopers on the back or shake them by the hands.'*

To Fight the Boers –N.S.W. Lancers Leave – *London Daily Chronicle*, 11 October 1899

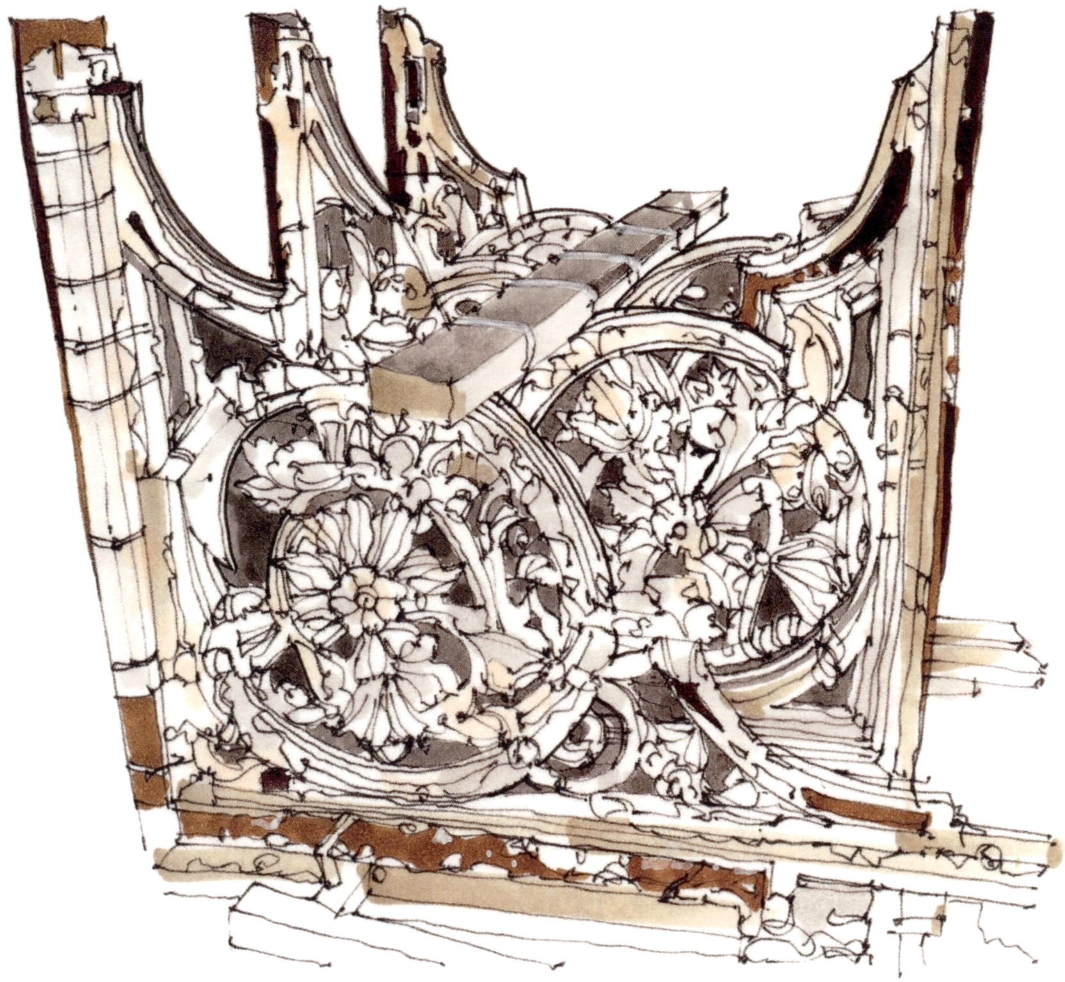

## FENCHURCH STREET STATION

One of the original London Monopoly railway stations and available for the princely sum of £200, Fenchurch Street was also one of the locations where the game maker Waddingtons held Monopoly championships in 1936 (on Platforms 3 and 4), such was the game's popularity at the time.

Just like other London terminuses, the station's popularity has left its marks in other places, too. Aside from Fenchurch in *The Hitchhiker's Guide to the Galaxy*, it makes a cameo appearance in the 2005 film *Green Street*, masquerading as Manchester Piccadilly (Journey 2), although how those two stations could be made to look alike is beyond me, and finally the ultimate accolade from the poet Sir John Betjeman, who refers to it in 1972 as 'the only untouched railway terminus left in London', when the floral, cast-iron spandrels could be seen in the station. The station also makes an appearance in Betjeman's book, *London's Historic Railway Stations*. Carrying on the literary theme, it was the site for the first railway station bookstall, set up by William Marshall, who supplied newspapers to the Great Western Railway.

Of course, the station is no longer 'untouched'; it was redeveloped between 1983–87, with the designs of Fitzroy Robinson Partnership, with engineers Ove Arup and Partners sitting behind the original 1841 facade. The new Grade II listed structure became the first fully 'buttwelded framed building', which meant platforms and concourse could have a clear span, unobstructed by columns, with five storeys of office accommodation above in anodized dark brown panelling. The original station was design by Sir William Tite (1798–1873) – also architect of the Royal Exchange in London, president of the Royal Institute of British Architects (RIBA) (twice) and a Member of Parliament – and in 1854 it was expanded by Sir George Berkley (1821–1893).

*(opposite) Ornate cast-iron spandrels from the old Fenchurch Street Station*

*(above) The Cheshire Cheese pub in the brick arches under Fenchurch Street Station*

*(above) The former Tilbury Riverside Station*
*(opposite) Tilbury Dock Cruise Terminal*

Fenchurch Street was the main terminus of the London & Blackwall Railway, originally masterminded by Robert Stephenson. There were originally six stations along the 5.6-km (3.5-mile) route between Fenchurch Street and Blackwall, which was carried on a brick viaduct between Minories and West India Docks.

Fenchurch Street Station was built above Crutched Friars and Savage Gardens, with a brick arch that was constructed in 1839, and extended to the north in 1881 with steel girders to support additional platforms. At street level the Cheshire Cheese public house replaced an inn from around 1600, although most of its features are now nineteenth century.

In 1865, the Great Eastern Railway took over these lines on a 999-year lease, as well as those to Tilbury and Southend, where we go on the rest of our journey.

### TILBURY RIVERSIDE & TILBURY DOCK CRUISE TERMINAL

Tilbury Riverside opened on 13 April 1854 and closed 138 years later on 30 November 1992. At its busiest, it had six platforms sitting next to London's main cruise ship terminal, which thousands arriving into the United Kingdom would have used to complete their journey into London.

The current building is Grade II* listed (the listing includes the floating landing stage). Together with the station, built in neo-Georgian style, and the cruise terminal, it is built in red-brown brick laid in English bond with rusticated corner edging, or quoining, and Portland stone. It was completed in 1924, by architect Sir Edwin Cooper (1874–1942) in his capacity as architect to the Port of London Authority. Cooper also designed Marylebone Town Hall and it is also said that he designed more buildings in the City of London than anyone since Christopher Wren; considering that the latter was responsible for fifty-four churches that would be an impressive achievement!

By 1947, 300 liners per year were visiting Tilbury bringing about 140,000 passengers. To aid passengers, there was a frequent ferry service that acted as a tender to the liners berthed in the Thames and carried three million passengers per year. The cruise terminal and the station are better known, however, for events in 1948, when the *HMT Empire Windrush* docked here carrying new arrivals from the Caribbean, who would have an important part to play in rebuilding the United Kingdom's post-war economy. I can only imagine what it would have been like to leave the blue skies of home in the West Indies to arrive in Tilbury, and take the train from Riverside to Fenchurch Street in a smog-ridden post-war London.

*Southend Victoria Station*

Travel patterns began to change in the second half of the twentieth century, and Tilbury Riverside was finally closed in 1992 and replaced with a bus service with the same frequency of the trains. Ironically, checking today's bus timetables, the 99 bus still stops at Tilbury Riverside, some thirty-two years later.

Fortunately, this part of our journey doesn't end with a rail replacement service, but with the news that the Tilbury on the Thames Trust, after nine years of hard work, has secured major funding for the Back on Track project. This aims to transform the railway station into an exciting space for arts, community events, socializing, 'enjoying a cup of coffee while watching the ships go by along the Thames, and celebrating its rich heritage, from the arrival of the *Empire Windrush* to its legacy as a key stop for cruise liners today and from a bygone era'. According to a 2024 promotional video, construction work was due to start imminently, with completion due in approximately two years.

## SOUTHEND VICTORIA

In 1854, Sir Samuel Morton Peto (Journey 4) leased the railway and completed the development of the Tilbury line to Southend, a magnet for holidaying Londoners, especially those from the East End. Train companies would lay on

special services and even advertise these in advance. It was the railways that made seaside towns such as Southend what they were. The *Southend Standard* of 1910 states:

*'By six o'clock in the evening the human tides begin to return to the railway stations and crowd the trains again. Much singing and dancing was there, not quite so clear and steady as in the morning, but nevertheless all good humoured.'*

Southend Victoria, a terminus on the Shenfield-Southend line, is a short walk from Southend Central, which itself is just over an hour's train ride from Fenchurch Street. Unusually, the stations on the Shenfield–Southend line are largely in their original form, including the platform canopies. These fifteen stations were designed in a 'domestic revival' style, pioneered by the Great Eastern Railway's architect, W. N. Ashbee (1852–1919). He was also the architect of Liverpool Street Station (Journey 4).

The first station on this site was built in 1889, and evolved to become Southend for Westcliffe & Thorpe Bay from 1933 to 1949, when it was renamed Southend-on-Sea Victoria, which was finally changed to its current name in 1969.

Just outside the station is a sculpture, *The Return*, by René Julien, which shows a couple embracing, presumably reunited after a journey to Southend Victoria, seeming like a less constrained version of the couple in *A Strange Meeting*.

## SOUTHEND CLIFF RAILWAY

One of the many sights in Southend would have been the Cliff Lift. This replaced the Electric Elevator, also known as the Revolving Stairway, which was a forerunner to the escalator, and was constructed in 1901 by the American engineer Jesse W. Reno (1861–1947). Noise and lack of reliability due to exposure to the elements meant a decision was taken to replace it in 1911.

The current lift, opened on August Bank Holiday in 1912, is a funicular railway constructed by the American company, Waygood & Co. (now part of Otis), and operates on a slope of 43.4 per cent with a 1.37-m- (4ft 6-in-) gauge. There have been three renovations, in 1930, 1959 and 1990. In 2003, a serious problem resulted in the lift being out of action for seven years until service was restored with the help of Heritage Lottery Funding and reopened in 2010.

## SOUTHEND PIER RAILWAY

A seaside holiday is usually only complete when some time has been spent on the pier. The original pier in Southend opened in 1830, followed in 1889 by the iron pier, which was designed by Sir James Brunlees (1816–92), a Scottish civil engineer. He was also responsible for the Ulverstone & Lancaster Railway, a short but important railway to link Furness Railway to the Lancaster and Carlisle line (Journey 9) and on to all points further south in the British

network. He even worked as far afield as Brazil on the São Paulo Railway and in New Zealand.

The end of the pier has been extended several times, with the Prince George Extension that opened in 1929 bringing the length of the pier to 2.14km (1.33 miles), making it the longest pier in the UK. In 2023, Southend Pier won the National Piers Society's Pier of the Year Award.

However, it is really the railway on the pier that is the reason for its inclusion. The very first mode of transport along the pier was a horse-drawn tramway in 1872. A single-track electric railway arrived in 1890, making it the first pier railway in the country. By 1930–31, four trains were running on double tracks. The two eco-friendly trains are now named *Sir William Heygate* and *Sir David Amess*, following a name change from Sir John Betjeman to the former local MP.

What would Fenchurch have made of our journey and particularly of Southend? Her book character doesn't exactly share her thought on this particular subject, but given that Arthur Dent and his shipmate Ford Prefect remarked that looking out from the *Heart of Gold* everything looked like Southend, she would have probably thought that the improbability drive was rather fond of piers with railways on.

*(opposite) Southend Cliff Railway*
*(above) Southend Pier Railway*

JOURNEY

# 4

# ROYAL RAILWAYS

## WOLFERTON *to* LIVERPOOL STREET

WOLFERTON

KING'S LYNN

BURY ST EDMUNDS SIGNAL BOX

NEEDHAM MARKET

REEDHAM SWING BRIDGE

NORWICH

LIVERPOOL STREET

Embark on a historic railway journey through architectural grandeur, royal elegance and industrial legacy. From Wolferton's Tudor charm, hosting royal guests en route to Sandringham, to King's Lynn boasting a café, unchanged for over a century and Bury St Edmunds Signal Box, an iconic GER design painted in cheerful yellow and green, a relic of mechanical railway communication. Next, marvel at the engineering of Reedham Swing Bridge and Norwich's palatial Thorpe Station before concluding at Liverpool Street, a true cathedral of railways.

## WOLFERTON

Originally named Wolverton in 1862, but renamed Wolferton a year later, this first stop was built for the Royal Family on the Sandringham estate. The station, described by Sir John Betjeman as 'different from all other stations in England', features in a brilliant film, *John Betjeman Goes by Train* in the BFI film archive made by British Transport Films in collaboration with BBC East Anglia in 1962. Over a ten-minute programme, it describes a journey from the town of King's Lynn to the seaside resort of Hunstanton, during which Betjeman travels through Wolferton, highlighting the way the buildings have been designed to blend into the surroundings, with no posters, and the signal box matching the adjacent cottage.

The Grade II* listed buildings are of Tudor appearance in brick, half-timbered with rendered panels under a plain tiled roof, designed under the guidance of W. N. Ashbee to create a series of Royal reception and retiring rooms. You can almost imagine the Royal Family and their guests waiting, as they travelled to Sandringham, for their luggage to be transported to the Royal Residence, during which time, 'Gentlemen would have a drink and a smoke in King Edward's room, while the ladies would take tea in Queen Alexandra's room, or, possibly, her garden'. The station closed in 1969 with the then Queen commenting that 'King's Lynn would be Sandringham House's nearest railhead.'

The buildings have changed hands numerous times in the past few decades, but are open to the public and operate as a museum. Bressingham Steam Museum also owns two of the former Royal Coaches, Nos. 396 and 2901, which were used by Queen Elizabeth II and the Duke of Edinburgh, Prince Charles and various royal staff throughout their life and offers a fascinating insight on how the royal railways operated, complete with food menus.

**W. N. ASHBEE & SIR SAMUEL MORTON PETO**
(1852–1919 & 1809–89)

The two men featured in this journey were critical in the creation of its railway infrastructure in the latter half of the nineteenth century. William Neville Ashbee for designing them and Sir Samuel Morton Peto for funding them.

Ashbee was the son of a stationmaster on the Great Western Railway and responsible for the design of Wolferton, Norwich and Liverpool Street Station as well as creating the 'domestic revival' style on the Shenfield to Southend line in the previous chapter. Both Norwich Station and the Shenfield to Southend line were projects that Peto also funded, so we can assume the two men not only met, but also knew each other reasonably well.

Ashbee headed up the architectural department of the Great Eastern Railway from 1883, a post he held until 1916. His major early work in the role was the impressive, chateau-like Norwich Thorpe station, built between 1884–86 in Renaissance style. Ashbee was also responsible for the design of Wolferton, the first station in this journey, built for the Royal Family in 1898 in a mainly domestic, Tudor style. He also worked as architect for the 1894 expansion of our terminus station, Liverpool Street, also built in a neo-Tudor style.

Peto was a more colourful character. An industrialist, philanthropist – he backed the Great Exhibition of 1851 – and MP, he was also a developer, mainly of railway infrastructure; among the projects he was responsible for are Curzon Street in Birmingham, the Great Western Railway and, in 1847 he also extended the Great Eastern Railway from Norwich to Lowestoft. Alongside his cousin Thomas Grissell, he was also involved in the construction of many other notable buildings, including the Lyceum Theatre, Nelson's Column, Woolwich Docks, and even the rebuilding of the Houses of Parliament after the fire of 1834, when the partnership was dissolved in *c.* 1846/47.

Peto was made a baronet for his war efforts funding the construction of the Grand Crimean Central Railway in 1855 to transport supplies to the troops at the front line during the Crimean War. He also continued to work internationally. building and promoting railways in Norway, Denmark, Canada, France, Australia, Algeria, Russia and Argentina.

While having its rewards, funding infrastructure, particularly the railways, has always had its risks and in 1866 Peto became bankrupt, partly due to the insolvency of the London, Chatham & Dover Railway. His reputation never recovered and despite prominent supporters such as Disraeli, he gave up his seat as an MP. Both men left an important legacy that reflects in our railways today.

*'. . . [He] would not yield to any man in his respect for the Sabbath; but they were dealing with this question upon public grounds, and in all cases where railways were involved, in testing the right of the public to use them, they could only be viewed as the public communication of the country.'*

Sir Samuel Morton Peto, House of Commons Debate on Sunday Travelling on Railways, 25 April 1849

*(opposite) Wolferton Station*

## KING'S LYNN

If the line were still working, it would take ten minutes to go from Wolferton to King's Lynn. Grade II listed, it looks markedly different to our royal station with its use of dark-blue colour on white wooden panels and white gault, red brick and partly glazed slate roofs. If Wolferton is domestic Tudor architecture, King's Lynn announces itself as sun-drenched summer holidays to be spent on the banks of the River Ouse or in the historic town centre.

The first station, which was wooden and basic, was opened in 1846 on the site of the goods yard. This was replaced by the current building constructed by Robert Skipper of Dereham in 1872, and was significantly extended in 1910. King's Lynn is a single-storey terminus station with the main building across the tracks, the concourse with a parallel roof behind this across the head of the platforms and two main platforms with buildings becoming islands with outer bay platforms, only one of which is still in use.

Interestingly, Robert Skipper's son, George Skipper (1856–1948), even though he didn't design any railway infrastructure, went on to become a leading architect in Norfolk in his own right and was responsible for the design of cottages for King George V at Sandringham, as well as the Royal Arcade, Jarrolds department store and Surrey House, amongst others in Norwich. Clearly, there must have been something in the genes as his brother, Frederick Wilemer Skipper, his uncle, Eric Haywood Skipper, and his son, Edward Goodwin Skipper, were all architects. At a retrospective of his work in 1974, Betjeman wrote, 'He is to Norwich rather what Gaudi was to Barcelona.'

Inside the station is one of the oldest and least altered cafés on the railway network, the Country Line Café. It is a timber buffet with central bay window, a panelled dado and

*(opposite) Country Line Cafe inside King's Lynn Station*

*(below) King's Lynn Station entrance*

more panelling above a modillion cornice. Opened in 1910, it not only celebrated the centenary of its opening in 2010, but in 2024 reached the final three in the World Cup of Stations (which celebrates the train station with the best local business) against cafés in Maghull and Dorridge.

## BURY ST EDMUNDS SIGNAL BOX

The number of signal boxes peaked at around 12–13,000 for Great Britain in the early part of the twentieth century. Now, nearly 100 years after their zenith, the number in operation is fewer than 100 as the mechanical levers are now replaced with digital signalling.

Built in approximately 1888 for the Great Eastern Railway, the Bury St Edmunds signal box is designated Grade II, but was decommissioned in 2017. The rather cheerful colour scheme of creamy yellow and green are actually the Great Eastern Railway colours and it is a particularly fine and large example of a Great Eastern Railway Type 7 design, which was built from 1885 until 1923. It is constructed of timber except for the red brick south-west corner with a slate-clad roof.

## NEEDHAM MARKET

Another stop on the Ipswich to Bury railways is Needham Market, which lies 124km (77 miles) down the line and nearly an hour and a half away from Liverpool Street.

Upon its opening in 1849, the *Illustrated London News* noted: 'It is an Elizabethan building, substantially constructed of red and white Suffolk bricks, the string-courses and cornices being of Caen stone, and the roofs covered with fancy tiles in patterns, and ornamental ridge crest ... Mr. Frederick Barnes, of Ipswich, is the architect of this very pleasing structure, as well as of the other stations on the line.'

The architect Frederick Barnes (1814–98) made his name designing buildings in Ipswich and railway stations in East Anglia, including Bury St Edmunds and Ipswich Stoke Hill, the latter of which has since made way for housing.

## REEDHAM SWING BRIDGE

Reedham is one of three swing bridges in East Anglia, all dating to around 1905. Built on the site of a Victorian swing bridge, it carries the Wherry Line between Norwich and Lowestoft over the River Yare, close to Reedham Station.

The original bridge was commissioned in the 1840s by none other than Sir Samuel Morton Peto to allow boats that were too tall to pass under conventional bridges for his Norwich to Lowestoft line. The bridge today has its own special signal box, which dates to 1904; it underwent substantial maintenance by Network Rail in 2022 and on average is opened 1,300 times per annum.

## NORWICH

Norwich initially boasted three stations: Thorpe station, which dates back to 1844 and was also the terminus of the Yarmouth to Norwich line, whose chairman was none other than George Stephenson, and its chief engineer being his son, Robert Stephenson; the second, Norwich Victoria (to the south-west of Thorpe), opened in 1849 and closed in 1916; and finally, Norwich City (north-west of our current station), closed in 1959. Now only Thorpe Station remains.

The current station, built in 1886, is where both Ashbee, as architect, working with Great Eastern Railway's chief engineer, John Wilson (1846–1922), and Peto, as contractor,

*(opposite) Bury St Edmunds' Signal Box*

*(above) Needham Market Station*

REEDHAM SWING BRIDGE

*Reedham Swing Bridge*

Norwich Station
M&S
P

*(below) Norwich Station entrance*

*(opposite) Detail of pediment above station windows with carved acanthus leaves*

came together. It is built of brick and stucco and overlooking the concourse is John Pooler's modern bust (1989) of Sir Samuel Morton Peto, who also represented the constituency as an MP from 1847–54.

Grade II listed, it isn't just the exterior, with its leaded dome or decorative curved pediments that contain acanthus leaves above its windows (which could be mistaken for the town hall of a major city), but also the interiors. Described by Historic England as having 'pilasters, decorated frieze cornice and plasterwork ceiling', the classical interior of the ticket office wouldn't look out of place in a building designed by Robert Adam. The platforms are also impressive and contain cast-iron columns with blue bases; capitals run the length of the platform with filigree decorative brackets that support the canopies.

*Interior of Liverpool Street Station*

## LIVERPOOL STREET

Liverpool Street Station, which serves around eighty million passengers every year, celebrated its 150th birthday in 2024. The sense of openness and light in the main concourse is striking and the atmospheric warm yellow filtered light over the platform make it seem as if you are about to embark on a magical journey. I didn't know when I first experienced it as a child that nearly forty years later it would become Britain's busiest train station due to the opening of Transport for London's Elizabeth line in 2022.

Opened in 1874 as a replacement for Bishopsgate Station, which no longer had the necessary capacity, Liverpool Street Station was designed to be more central and to integrate with the growing London Underground network and to serve routes from King's Lynn and Norwich.

The original core of the station was designed by Great Eastern Railway's chief engineer Edward Wilson (1820–77) and built by the firm of Lucas Brothers, which was founded by Charles Thomas Lucas (1820–95) and Thomas Lucas (1822–1902). Their contracts included the Royal Opera House in Covent Garden, the Royal Albert Hall and York Railway Station (Journey 11) and, in one final connection, the company worked on the construction of the Norwich & Brandon Railways by none other than Sir Samuel Morton Peto, who then asked Charles Lucas to rebuild his house Somerleyton Hall in Suffolk.

W. N. Ashbee designed the station's 1895 extension giving it the overall feel of a Gothic cathedral to trains, with its yellow-stock-and-red brickwork and pointed cast-iron arches spanning across the platforms. The remodelling of the station between 1985 and 1992 was undertaken by the British Rail Architects' Department under project lead Nick Derbyshire. The station itself is Grade II listed and the Great Eastern Station Hotel designed by Charles Barry is designated Grade II*. Liverpool Street was heavily bombed during both World Wars and also houses two memorials, one to the Kindertransport rescue mission during the Second World War, and the other to the Great Eastern Railway war memorial that commemorates the 1,000 employees who died in the First World War.

LiverpoolStreetStation
Lift

greateranglia

*Platform in Liverpool Street Station*

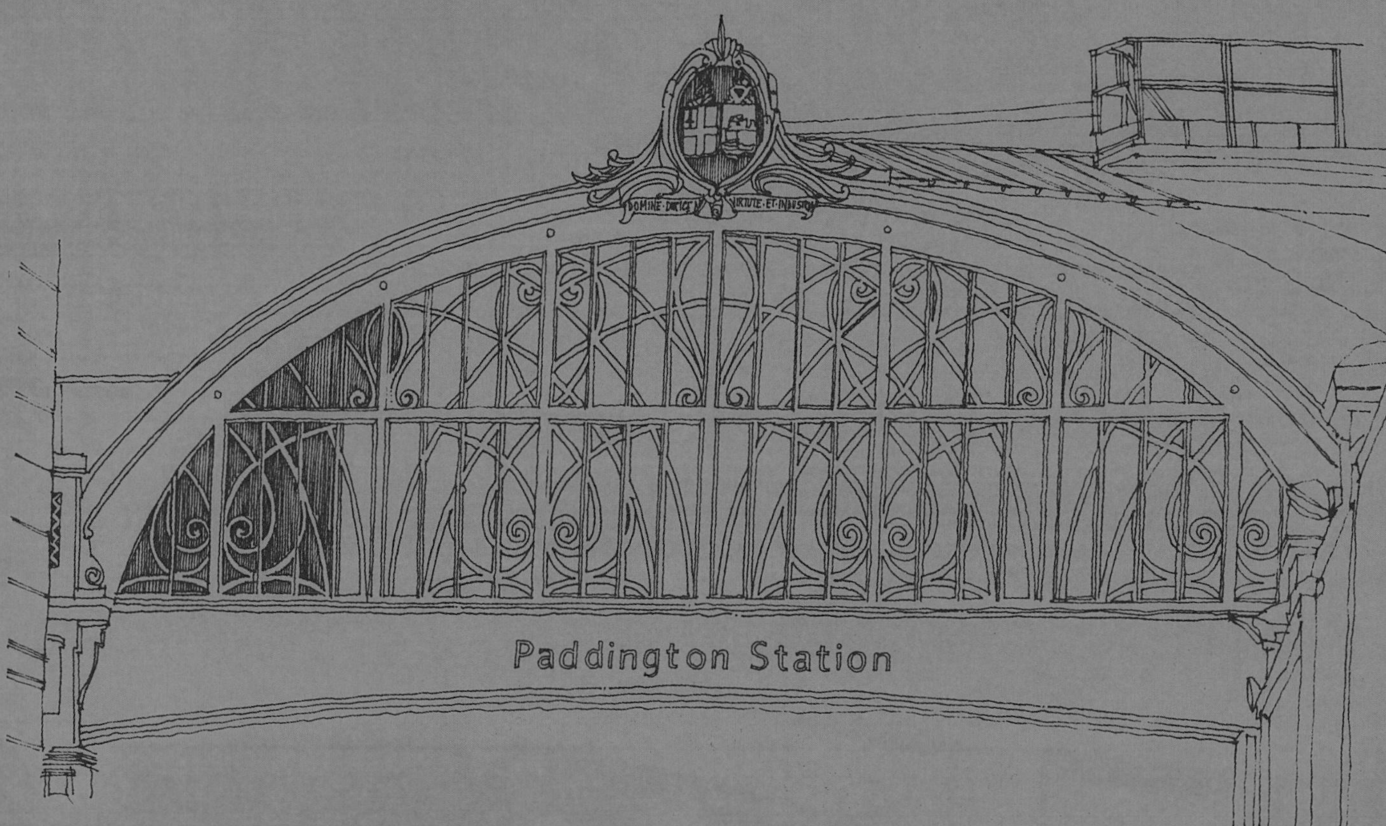
Paddington Station

JOURNEY

# 5

# GOING WEST

## PADDINGTON *to* ST IVES

PADDINGTON

BATH SPA

BRISTOL TEMPLE MEADS

NEWTON ABBOT

TORQUAY

THE ROYAL ALBERT BRIDGE

ST IVES TREGENNA CASTLE HOTEL

The journey from Paddington to St Ives highlights Isambard Kingdom Brunel's engineering genius, showcasing Victorian innovation through tunnels, tracks, stations and bridges. We start from Paddington's wrought-iron roof to Bath Spa's 'Tudorbethan' limestone station and then into Bristol Temple Meads where Gothic and Jacobean elements are crowned by Brunel's original train shed. The Royal Albert Bridge exemplifies structural mastery, leading to St Ives Tregenna Castle, its stately Georgian facade marking a grand conclusion.

GWR

*'I am going to design, in a great hurry, and I believe to build a station after my own fancy; that is, with engineering roofs, etc. etc. It is at Paddington, in cutting, and admitting of no exterior, all interior and all roofed in... Now such a thing will be entirely metal as to all the general forms, arrangements and design; it almost of necessity becomes an Engineering Work, but, to be honest, even if it were not, it is a branch of architecture of which I am fond.'*

Isambard Kingdom Brunel writing to Sir Matthew Digby Wyatt on Paddington, 1851

**PADDINGTON**

Brunel was strongly influenced by the Crystal Palace built to house the Great Exhibition of 1851. This can be clearly seen in his use of wrought iron and glass in the three-span roof at Paddington, at the time the largest train-shed roof in the world, with a main span (31.25m/102ft 6in) and two smaller ones to the north (21.3m/70ft) and south (20.7m/68ft). The station decoration, including the iron tracery with the 'moresque note' on the train-shed screens, was provided by Sir Matthew Digby Wyatt (1820–77), Brunel's architect on the project and also the executant architect of the Crystal Palace. Wyatt, a member of the architectural establishment, worked on a number of significant buildings, including one of my own personal favourites, the Durbar Court in the Foreign, Commonwealth and Development Office.

Fox Henderson & Company, which was also employed by Joseph Paxton (1803–65) to build Crystal Palace, was contracted to build the station. Sir Charles Fox (1810–74), one of the founders of the firm, later went into partnership with his sons, the firm being known as Sir Charles Fox and Sons, which today is part of Hyder Consulting.

The station that we know now dates back to 1854, but a temporary station was first on the site, while Paddington received its most significant visitor, Queen Victoria in 1842,

*(opposite) Train drawing into the platform at Paddington Station, with the Director's Balcony*

*(above) Statue of Brunel facing the Director's Balcony on Platform 1*

*Bath Spa Station*

when she made her first railway journey from Paddington to Slough (Windsor Castle) (Journey 6). Fifty years later, the last broad gauge express trains departed from Paddington marking the end of the Great Western Railway broad gauge.

Paddington has been remodelled and enlarged a further three times since its construction; first at the beginning of the First World War, then between 1930–35 and most recently, to accommodate Crossrail (2009–22).

Before moving on from Paddington, we should pay our respects to a famous statue. This is not Paddington Bear, who resides on Platform 1 with his own green memorial plaque, bench and shop, but sculptor John Doubleday's 1982 statue of Brunel , who faces the Director's Balcony on Platform 1, between Platforms 8 and 9.

## BATH SPA

An hour and a quarter down Brunel's line from Paddington brings us to Bath Spa Station, also designed by Brunel and opened in 1840. The station, now Grade II* listed, is built mainly of limestone ashlar. Its front entrance has three 'Flemish' gables above; the central gable's blue clock face with Roman numerals is a Gent 'Pulsynetic' electro/mechanical type (currently out for restoration). The design of the station is described by Historic England as 'Tudorbethan' and similar in style to Bristol Temple Meads.

Inside the station, the wider-than-usual spacing between the platforms is due to the broad gauge that Brunel used. Sadly, nothing remains of the original hammerbeam ceiling that spanned the platform, which was removed in 1897

Bristol Temple Meads

(although a similar architectural language can be seen at our next station). There is a final quirk that did survive in the station – a Victorian hydraulic lift.

## BRISTOL TEMPLE MEADS

The first proposal for a Bristol to London Railway was made in 1824, under the chairmanship of Thomas Wilson, MP. The first company was unable to raise funding, and it took until 1833 for there to be a viable proposition. In August 1833 the new company adopted the title of 'Great Western Railway' and appointed Isambard Kingdom Brunel their engineer.

The original Bristol Station, which was in a similar Tudorbethan style to both the original Paddington and Bath Spa stations, sits alongside the station in use today and was opened in August 1840. Temple Meads was expanded in the 1870s by Sir Francis Fox (1844–1927) (son of Sir Charles Fox) and in the first half of the 1930s by Percy Emerson Culverhouse. As a result of these expansions and additions, the Grade I listed station has a mixture of styles; part Palace of Westminster High Gothic, part Jacobean with the 1930s platforms and the cream tiling reminiscent of a suburban Underground station. Despite the melange of architecture, the station is impressive with its different scales and materiality, from the brick-and-sandstone-arched entrance corridor and expanse of the train shed, to even the small details such as the lead animals on the roof and of course a second statue of Brunel.

Next door to the current station is the original Brunel train shed, which operated for 125 years until its closure in 1965. The mock hammerbeam roof was built of wood as a nod to Westminster Hall in Whitehall, London and can still be seen as part of the car park at today's station.

It is in the 1870s that a misattribution occurred as to who actually designed the expanded Bristol Temple Meads. It had been long thought that this was Sir Matthew Digby Wyatt, who had also worked with Brunel on Paddington. This assumption went unchallenged until a few years ago when David Martyn, a local Bristol architect did some research and came across a final bill for design work for Temple Meads for £500, which was from Henry Lloyd (c.1813–87), as well as his original drawings of the scheme discovered at Brunel Institute. However, it seems that Lloyd's claim was rejected by the station's committee and he was forgotten until 2020

BRISTOL
Bristol Temple Meads
Customer
Lift

when the papers came to light. At the time of writing both the Historic England listing and the Network Rail summary for Temple Meads cite Wyatt, but hopefully Lloyd will receive the credit he deserves.

## NEWTON ABBOT

The current station, opened in 1927, is the most recent on our route. It was designed by Percy Emerson Culverhouse (1871–1953), Great Western Railway's chief architect (who also did the concourse of Cardiff Central). The original station was opened in 1846 by the South Devon Railway Company as its line was extended from Teignmouth. The route was extended a year later to Totnes in 1847 and a year after that to our next station, Torquay. All used Brunel's broad gauge.

Another of Brunel's innovations could be seen from the opposite side of the line; this was the pumping station for his 'atmospheric railway' that powered the train for a part of the route using differential air pressure. Atmospheric-operated railway services to Newton Abbott began on 17 December 1847 and from 23 February 1848 almost all trains ran atmospherically to this station. However, by May 1848 technical failures in the machinery were mounting; by September the atmospheric railway was abandoned.

## TORQUAY

The first station serving Torquay (which opened in 1848) was not long lived. Situated on a hill away from the centre of town and the harbour, it was inconvenient, and a new station was opened in 1878 in the current location, a mere ten minutes further down the line.

*(opposite) Tiled platform at Bristol Temple Meads*

*(above) Newton Abbot Station*

### ISAMBARD KINGDOM BRUNEL
(1806–59)

I have often wondered whether you can tell something about the psyche of a nation from the objects and people on its banknotes. If that is genuinely the case, then attachment to railways must run deep in the United Kingdom. Not only did George Stephenson appear on the old £5 notes up to 2003, but Isambard Kingdom Brunel featured on a specimen banknote in 1989, and perhaps it's only a matter of time before he appears permanently on one. After all, in the BBC's *100 Greatest Britons* series in 2002, Brunel was voted the second-greatest Briton ever, after Winston Churchill.

Born in 1806 in Portsea, son of one of the eminent engineers of the Industrial Revolution, Marc Brunel (1769–1849), Isambard studied both in France and in the United Kingdom. His first job and apprenticeship was spent at his father's practice, working mainly on the Thames Tunnel. In 1828, he was badly injured when flooding destroyed a substantial amount of the tunnel and was sent to recuperate in Bristol. It was during this time that he designed and later won the competition to build the Clifton Suspension Bridge, a project that was only eventually completed as a tribute to Brunel after his death.

The design and construction of the Great Western Railway, which we follow here, was all-consuming for Brunel. You can see his legacy in every aspect of this route: from the design of Paddington Station, to every viaduct, tunnel, embankment, sea defence, and then to the Royal Albert Bridge that crosses the River Tamar into Cornwall. The other major innovation was Brunel's development of a broad gauge track – 2,140mm (7ft ¼in) broader than the standard 1,435mm (4ft 8½in). It argued that with this broader gauge, locomotives could travel at 97km/h (60mph) rather than 56km/h (35mph), due to the lower centre of gravity making the carriages more stable and the train run faster. Despite the science behind Brunel's broad gauge it eventually lost out to Stephenson's narrower one – the majority ruled.

At his death in 1859, fellow engineer Daniel Gooch (1816–89) commented: 'By his death the greatest of England's engineers was lost, the man with the greatest originality of thought and power of execution, bold in his plans, but right', a very apt epitaph for a man who had a lasting impact on Britain's transport network through the construction of over 100 bridges, 25 railway lines –including the journey in this chapter – docks, tunnels and even three ships.

*The approach to the Royal Albert Bridge*

*(above) Torquay Station*
*(opposite) St Ives Tregenna Castle Hotel*

The Grade II listed station was designed and built by Great Western Railway architect and engineer J. E. Danks (1843–1910) and William Lancaster-Owen (1843–1911), assisted by the engineers Vernon and Ewens of Cheltenham. Torquay and the journey to it is one of the first main railway journeys I took with my parents when I first arrived in this country. Its distinctive French looks, both austere and squat fairytale chateau, with its rock-faced grey limestone facade and lace iron tops, and the two mini towers either side of the track, have stayed with me.

## THE ROYAL ALBERT BRIDGE

Another hour and a half later and on the Cornish Main Line Railway towards St Ives, we are going over the Royal Albert Bridge. Designed in 1852, it was opened on 2 May 1859, four months before Brunel died, by Prince Albert. After Brunel's death, the Cornwall Railway Company decided to make the bridge a memorial to him by adding the words *I.K. BRUNEL, ENGINEER, 1859* in large metal letters on either end.

The bridge crosses the River Tamar at its narrowest point of 335m (1,100ft) at Saltash, and the two-span (each span being 139m/455ft) bowstring suspension bridge allows a clearance of 30m (100ft) above mean high water to allow for sailing ships to pass underneath without difficulty.

The spans each have a wrought-iron tubular arch in the shape of a parabola, with suspension chains hung either side of the tube in a curve. Working together with the tube's rise, which is the same as the dip of the chains, a structural system is created where forces are all contained in the bridge. The principle is the same as a suspension bridge, making the Royal Albert Bridge the only bridge of that type that carries main line trains. The bridge was Grade I listed in 1952.

### ST IVES TREGENNA CASTLE HOTEL

Just over two hours later via Plymouth and then St Erth, we arrive at St Ives. This time, the focus isn't on the station but the Tregenna Castle Hotel. Today it might be best known as the hotel resort that hosted the G7 summit in the middle of Covid pandemic in 2021, but it has a 250-year history since its construction in 1774 as private residence for a wealthy Cornishman. The architect is thought to be John Wood the Younger (1728–82), the Bath architect who also designed the Royal Crescent and the Assembly Rooms.

Nearly a century later, it was sold to a family of local bankers. They then leased and eventually sold it to the Great Western Railway in 1895, the hotel becoming a 'jewel in the crown' of their railway hotels. You can imagine it would have been the perfect place for a First Class passenger, disembarking from the train at St Ives, to be driven up to the top of the cliff to stay in one's own castle with about 28 hectares (70 acres) of grounds and remarkable views.

The castle hotel also gave its name to a Castle Class locomotive, *Tregenna Castle No. 5006*. There was fierce competition internationally for the title of fastest locomotive and the Paddington to Cheltenham route was recognized as one of the quickest. On 6 June 1932 Tregenna Castle, driven by Harry Ruddock and Harry Thorp, set a new record covering the 124.4km (77.3 miles) between Swindon and Paddington in 56 minutes and 47 seconds, at an average speed of 124.4km/h (81.6mph) and, in one part of the journey over 145km/h (90mph). Today the commuter service takes between 50–56 minutes with one stop!

JOURNEY

# 6

# WALES

## BARMOUTH *to* PADDINGTON

BARMOUTH

ABERYSTWYTH

SHREWSBURY STATION &
SEVERN BRIDGE SIGNAL BOX

SWANSEA

CARDIFF

NEWPORT

PADDINGTON

The Cambrian Line narrates a story of architectural and engineering mastery. From Barmouth's Grade II* viaduct, Britain's longest wooden railway bridge, to Aberystwyth's ashlar-fronted station with its clock tower, these structures blend functionality with elegance. Shrewsbury's Tudor-Gothic grandeur transitions into Swansea's and Cardiff's 1930s GWR art-deco elegance, in contrast to Newport's glass and steel. Finally, the journey culminates in Paddington, a Victorian masterpiece reminiscent of Crystal Palace.

*Barmouth Viaduct*

## BARMOUTH

The Cambrian line today covers a large part of Wales. Our starting point is on the west coast, in Barmouth, home to the Barmouth Viaduct. It is a Grade II* listed structure constructed by the Aberystwyth and Welsh Coast Railway in 1867. The 770-m (2,525-ft) structure is by some way the longest viaduct in Wales (and the oldest still in use in the country), as well as the longest wooden railway bridge in Britain. When built, the bridge included a lift span to allow tall ships to pass. In 1906, three fixed and two swinging metallic spans were installed, carried on cast-iron cylinders.

The viaduct recently completed a four-year renovation and restoration project during which the bridge was only fully closed for a total of thirteen weeks. Some statistics courtesy of Network Rail that underline the scale of the work undertaken include:

- Over 70m (230ft) of rock anchors
- Over 40 tonnes (44.8 tons) of cast in-situ concrete
- Over 400 tonnes (448 tons) of new steel and 150 tonne (168 tons) of temporary steelwork

This amount of temporary and new steel work is the equivalent of twice the weight of the Statue of Liberty, or approximately 400 female hippopotamuses!

**ABERYSTWYTH**

Our next stop on the Cambrian Line is Aberystwyth, two and a half hours and a change at Dovey Junction later. The railway station was opened in 1864 as the terminus for the Aberystwyth & Welsh Coast Railway, which later became part of Cambrian Railways. The 1920s station building is a classical two-storey structure, like a town hall you might build for an affluent town. The 1924–25 a new station building was designed by Harris and Sheppard, ashlar-fronted with a square clock tower to the east end with four clock faces.

Unfortunately, the station has declined and contracted since the sixties. Its goods facilities and all sidings were removed; the signal box and goods shed were demolished and the site of the yard and carriage sidings sold for redevelopment, while the station building from the twenties is now used as a Wetherspoon pub. It is good to note, however, that the old platform signs can still be seen as part of the fabric of the pub and that it got a National Railway Heritage award from Network Rail for its conversion in 2003.

**SHREWSBURY STATION & SEVERN BRIDGE SIGNAL BOX**

Shrewsbury Station was opened in 1849 and designed by architect Thomas Mainwaring Penson (1818–64), who was also responsible for a number of stations in the

Aberystwyth Station

**DAVID DAVIES**
(1818–90)

David Davies, born in 1818, played a pivotal role in the development of railways in Mid Wales. He established the first railway connection between Newtown and Llanidloes in 1859, despite these towns not being connected to any other railway at the time. He built over 230km (145 miles) of track and tackled major projects like the Talerddig Cutting. Davies later became managing director of Cambrian Railways, with Llanidloes Station serving as the company's headquarters from 1864. Cambrian Railways eventually merged with the Great Western Railway in 1922. His work laid the foundation for further industrial developments in Wales.

*'About the time of his marriage, he undertook to construct a railway between Llanidloes and Newtown. Though the company's intention was to let the work out in small contracts, he felt a strong desire to undertake the whole work himself. He walked over the ground several times, counted the cost, undertook the work, finished it to the satisfaction of the company, and made a substantial profit to himself for his labour. As there was not at that time another railroad in the whole of North Wales, the difficulties he had to contend with were very great. All the leading features of his character were displayed in accomplishing this work, namely, quick perception, correct judgment, inexhaustible energy, great courage, and a generous heart.'*

Portrait and Biographical Sketch of the Late David Davies – *The Christian Standard*, November 1891

Welsh Marches. His father Thomas Penson (1790–1859) became county surveyor for Montgomeryshire in 1817, and of Denbighshire in 1819. He was also surveyor for the Montgomeryshire Turnpike Trusts and took an active interest in the proposed new Welsh railways.

The building is unusual, in that the station was later extended in 1901 by the construction of a new floor underneath the original station building. The station's platforms also extend over the River Severn. Its three-storey, Tudor-Gothic style, ashlar faced with a Welsh slate roof, was apparently influenced by an Oxbridge college, embellished with a central clock tower, castellations, and mullion windows.

The station allegedly also has its own ghost. In the winter of 1888, a local councillor was crushed to death when the ornate glass roof gave way under the weight of the snow and killed him, and his ghost is said to hang around Platform 3 waiting for a train to London.

The station is also the site of the Shrewsbury rail accident, which occurred on 15 October 1907. An overnight sleeping-car and mail train from Manchester to the West of England derailed on the sharply curved approach to the station, killing eighteen people and injuring many (accounts vary as to the number of injuries being between thirty-three and sixty-one). The accident was concluded to be due to excessive speed on a dangerous curve.

*(opposite) Shrewsbury Station, front facade*

*(top) Commemorative headlamp made for Queen Victoria's jubilee in 1897*

*(above) Five Seats notice from the Science Museum collection showing the number of casualties from the Shrewsbury Rail disaster*

A detailed report by the investigator Lt-Col H. A. Yorke and photographs of the accident can be found in the Railway Archives, and the tragedy is commemorated in the plaque in the Science Museum collection from the London & North Western Railway, with a 'Five Seats' notice attached, inscribed '18 killed 44 injured. Shrewsbury Railway Disaster. Oct 15th 1907'. It is unclear why this inscription was made on a 'Five Seats' notice, which shows the legal carrying capacity of a carriage or mode of transport, but I suspect it might have been the closest object to hand.

Just outside the station is the Severn Bridge Signal Box, the 120-year-old, Grade II listed building – the world's largest working mechanical signal box. It still has its original 180 levers inside, all dating from 1903. Eighty-nine of those levers are still used to signal about 280 trains every day. It also won the 2021 National Railway Heritage Award.

## SWANSEA

This station is the first and the last remaining of seven passenger terminus stations that once existed in Swansea. It was opened on 18 June 1850 by the South Wales Railway, whose line from Chepstow to Swansea was engineered by Isambard Kingdom Brunel. Almost 700 guests gathered to celebrate the line's opening.

In the Network Rail archives there are a number of nineteenth-century drawings as well as a contract witnessed by Brunel for the construction of the South Wales Railway. It was conceived as a broad-gauge railway to link the Gloucester & Dean Forest Railway with Neyland in Wales.

*(opposite) The Severn Bridge Signal Box*

*(above) The last remaining railway station in Swansea*

It also served the South Wales Valley, shipping coal to London and Ireland. It was part of Brunel's ambition to better link London and New York.

The route was due to travel from Fishguard and cross the River Severn just west of Gloucester. When the bridge at Chepstow was finished in July 1852, the connection to Gloucester and London was completed but, due to financial problems, construction of the line west of Swansea was delayed and the construction of the Irish railways that would connect with the Fishguard ferries at Waterford was abandoned. Swansea is now the terminus of regular services from London Paddington and an intermediate stop for hourly trains (which reverse at Swansea) between West Wales, Cardiff and Manchester.

In 1877–78 the station was completely rebuilt and in 1934–35 the current elevation was built by the Great Western Railways's in-house team in a style that was typical for the company in this period. Amusingly, as you leave the station, inscribed on the floor outside the entrance are the words 'Ambition is critical', a product of Swansea council's 1992 commissioning of local artists to produce poems about a sense of place. Poet David Hughes came up with 'Ambition is critical' as a riposte to an old saying that Swansea is the 'graveyard of ambition'.

## CARDIFF

The Grade II listed building is managed by Transport for Wales Rail, and is both the largest and busiest station in Wales. The route to this station is of course Brunel's and to

*(above) Cardiff Station*

*(opposite) Concourse and booking hall at Cardiff Station*

create the site for the station, he diverted the River Taff to the west, creating the larger and safer location where the station now stands.

The original station that was opened in 1850 was made of wood; the art-deco masonry structure that we use today was built in 1934 by Percy Emerson Culverhouse (1871–1953), Great Western Railway's chief architect from 1929 to 1945. During his tenure, he designed a large number of stations including Bath, Newton Abbot (Journey 5) and the thirties expansion of Bristol Temple Meads. For me, though, my favourite part of the station is the Portland-stone booking hall and concourse and its similarity with the one at Leeds Station. The stylized octagonal lights that hang from the panelled ceiling (replicas of the originals installed in 1999 with funding from the Railway Heritage Trust) make me dream of the bygone glamorous days of rail travel.

During recent renovation works to the clock tower of the station, one of the Network Rail team on site found a piece of old lead that was no longer needed, and made it into a dragon himself by hand. The rail company said the dragon will now 'quietly keep watch' over the station.

### NEWPORT

Newport Station might not be considered a classic beauty by many and was even nominated for the Carbuncle Cup (a prize given to the worst building in the country) in 2011, but it does have a touch of heroism about it with its panelled glazing, sweeping bridge over the platforms and glass roofs that show the Welsh sky. Designed in 2010 by the architects Grimshaw (also responsible for the new London Bridge Station) in association with the engineers Atkins, it has four full-size platforms that facilitate the Great Western Railway's ten-carriage Intercity Express

*A view from the platform of Newport Station*

Programme trains and is the second-busiest station in Wales after Cardiff. The architects themselves describe it as 'Architecturally, the station design takes its inspiration from the iconic domes of the Eden Project. The glass roofs flood the concourse with light, creating a spacious, contemporary feel.'

The station was originally opened in 1850 by the South Wales Railway Company and greatly expanded in 1928 and renamed Newport High Street. At one point there were ten railway stations in the city boundaries of Newport, underlining the importance of the city. Now only three remain, one in the city centre and two on the outskirts. The old railway station, which looks like a grander, elongated version of Newton Abbot, is now next door, having been converted to offices in 2011.

### PADDINGTON

An hour and 40 minutes later we are back at Paddington. We've already explored the architecture of this magnificent station in Journey 5, but there are some stories and elements that deserve a return trip.

If you're lucky as your train draws in to Paddington on a Friday evening you might be welcomed into London by the music of a brass band, and not just any brass band – the oldest and only surviving one in the railway network. The band takes a break in the winter months, (it gets too cold to play in the station between Christmas and Easter), but concerts usually start at 7.30 p.m. prompt and go on until 9.00 p.m. This incarnation of the band dates back to 1923, but it was actually around before that. They don't know how far back the band originally dates, but there are photos of it from 1910. It has gone through a few iterations. The previous, older band was The Great Western Railway and Paddington Borough Band, while the 1923 band was The Great Western Railway Staff Military Band. Despite the name, there are a number of band members who have never worked in the railway and they are always on the lookout for new talent.

Once you've listened to the band, perhaps you have some time before catching another train. On Platform 1, you can

find the old royal waiting room, which is now Great Western Railway's first-class lounge. Turn right from the main lounge area and you arrive at Queen Victoria's private waiting room at Paddington. There are still some original parts, like a framed section that shows the original decoration, old photographs of Paddington Station, railway posters and royal sigils. The waiting rooms were used by the Royal Family up until the beginning of the Second World War. During the War, they were used for a number of purposes, including as a first-aid facility and a storage area. Original photographs of what they used to look like can be found in the archive collection of the London Transport Museum.

You can almost imagine what it must have been like for Queen Victoria in the waiting room after she became the first British monarch to travel by train, making her historic thirty-minute maiden voyage from Slough to Paddington on 13 June 1842. In 1897, in commemoration of Queen Victoria's diamond jubilee, Great Western Railway made a locomotive headlamp – very appropriate for a queen whose last journey by train took place on Saturday, 2 February 1901, right at the end of her reign as part of her funeral cortege. For this, the Great Western Railway produced a special train plan for the *'Funeral of Her Late Most Gracious Majesty The Queen. Arrangement of Royal Train. Paddington to Windsor. 1.32 pm. Saturday 2 February 1901'.*

*(top) Paddington Station glazed screen on Praed Street*

*(opposite top) The brass band playing in Paddington Station on a Friday evening*

*(opposite bottom) Great Western Railway bench and original details from the ex-Royal now first-class waiting room at Paddington*

GWR
GWR

JOURNEY

7

# NORTH WALES

## HOLYHEAD *to* EUSTON

HOLYHEAD

BRITANNIA BRIDGE

BETWS-Y-COED

STOKE-ON-TRENT

COVENTRY

EUSTON

From Holyhead's celebrated iron clock to Britannia Bridge's tubular might, North Wales' railways embody industrial artistry and ambition. The journey from Betws-y-Coed, nestled in slate-laden Snowdonia, to Stoke-on-Trent, with its Jacobean grandeur and restored gothic fireplace, showcases Britain's evolving railway landscape. Coventry's modernist elegance contrasts and yet connects with our terminus at Euston, where its lost Doric Arch and Britannia Statue are symbols of heritage lost to time. United by history these stations weave a narrative of ambition and progress, bridging past and future seamlessly.

*Iron Clock outside Holyhead Station*

## HOLYHEAD

On arrival at Holyhead Station, you are greeted with a Grade II-listed iron clock painted white with black detailing, which stood here since 1880. Its inscription reads: 'Holyhead Old Harbour Extension works commenced January 1875. Opened by His Royal Highness The Prince of Wales 17th June 1880'. The clock is by J. B. Joyce & Co, which also made the clocks in Aberystwyth Station (Journey 6) and Liverpool Lime Street (Journey 2), as well as a number in cathedrals and even overseas as far afield as Sydney, Shanghai and Cape Town.

Moving on from timepieces, the first station here dates back to 1848, built by the Chester & Holyhead Railway and then replaced only three years later in 1851. The present station was opened by the London and North Western Railway on 17 January 1866 and is next to the port. It still retains its long curving train shed (also Grade II listed), which is considered to be the longest in Wales (approximately 300m/1000ft long), and is built in red brick with stone cornice and dressings, and string courses of moulded yellow brick.

## BRITANNIA BRIDGE

As parts of the country became being increasingly connected and rail travel more and more popular, a rail link was planned across the Menai Strait for MPs travelling to and from Ireland. The existing Menai Suspension Bridge was not deemed to be appropriate to have a railway line crossing it, and therefore a second bridge across the Strait was commissioned.

The foundations were laid in 1846 and the bridge was completed in 1850. It was designed by Robert Stephenson with architectural elements by Francis Thompson (1808–95), who became the architect for the North Midland Railway (NMR) in 1839 and designed stations in Chester, Derby (including the Roundhouse (Journey 11) and a further twelve stations for the NMR.

### J. B. JOYCE & CO AND THWAITES & REED (CLOCKMAKERS TO THE RAILWAYS)

(1690 & 1610)

Since the birth of the railways in 1825, clocks have played a critical role in timekeeping. Well into the first half of the nineteenth century, different towns and cities kept different local times, contrasting with railway timetables and clocks at stations along the expanding railway network, which displayed a standard 'mean' time set in London at the Royal Observatory, Greenwich. A consistent, standardized time was important not just for integrating the timetable and running a punctual service, but also for safety. The Great Western Railway brought in the first railway standardized time in 1840, and it was subsequently adopted by all other train operators. Greenwich Mean Time (GMT), as it was already widely known, became Britain's legal standard time in 1880.

Therefore, clocks and, more importantly, accurate clocks were an essential part of any railway station, which had them displayed in multiple locations, whether on a clock tower outside the building, inside in the booking hall and concourse or on the platforms. A number of these timepieces such the clocks at St Pancras, Waterloo, Darlington, York and Paddington, are still in situ and are prominent symbols of the railways. This chapter delves into some of these horological masterpieces and follows the history of two of the main makers, the Shropshire firm J. B. Joyce & Co of Whitchurch, which claims to be the oldest clock manufacturer in the world, originally established in 1690, and Thwaites & Reed, which contests this and claims to have been in continuous manufacture since before 1740, with antecedents back to 1610.

*'LONDON TIME is kept at all the Stations on the Railway, which is about 4 minutes earlier than READING time; 5½ minutes before STEVENTON time; 7½ minutes before CIRENCESTER time; 8 minutes before CHIPPENHAM time; 11 minutes before BATH and BRISTOL time; and 14 minutes before BRIDGEWATER time.'*

Timetable of the Great Western Railway line from London to Bridgewater, 1841

Like other bridges of this date it needed to be at least 30m (100ft) above the high water level to allow sailing ships to move unimpeded under it. Furthermore, it had to support two train tracks. The engineering challenge was given to Robert Stephenson, whose design team also included William Fairbairn (1789–1874), who succeeded George and Robert Stephenson as the third president of the Institution of Mechanical Engineers, and Eaton Hodgkinson (1789–1861), who proved mathematically that extra chains wouldn't be needed to support the bridge.

Letters in the Science Museum archive point to the difficulties faced in building the bridge, and a letter from Robert Stephenson to Captain Constantine Moorsom dated 10 March 1848 starts, 'Sir, the tides have been so rapid that it has been impossible to hold the Pontoon under the tubes . . . and away they go careering in every direction like wild beasts'.

Stephenson's design was for a tubular type of bridge with the railway line running through tubes made up of wrought-iron riveted plates. The two longest tubes were built in sections in Caernarfon, floated into position using pontoons, and then raised on to the towers using a hydraulic jack. Once in position, they were joined, making a beam of 460.5m (1,511ft), at the time the longest wrought-iron span in the world. At each corner of the bridge two lions were placed, sculpted by John Thomas (1813–62), also the sculptor of the statue of Britannia that used to sit in Euston Station.

Until a fire in 1970, the Britannia Bridge remained unaltered. It took four years for the bridge to then be reconstructed and in 1980, it was also adapted to take road traffic. The charred remains of part of the bridge can be seen in the Science Museum Collection with a painted inscription *LAST RIVET / MARCH 5 1850 / R.STEPHENSON.*

*Britannia Bridge over the Menai Strait*

## BETWS-Y-COED

It takes a couple of hours from Holyhead across the Britannia Bridge, with a change at Llandudno Junction, to arrive at the charming station of Betws-y-Coed. At the entrance we are welcomed by another clock, but this time a more modern one dated 2003, and right next door is the Conwy Valley Railway Museum. The station is also home to one of the oldest postboxes in Wales, dating back to 1857.

Betws-y-Coed's passenger trains began service on 6 April 1868. An Act of Parliament in 1865 had permitted the London & North Western Railway to extend the Conwy Valley line, and the Betws-y-Coed extension opened in 1867 for freight trains, primarily carrying slate out of Snowdonia.

The station building at Betws-y-Coed was constructed by local man Owen Gethin Jones (1816–83), originally a stonemason before branching out into carpentry and then civil engineering, though he was also known as a poet. He is commemorated by Pont Gethin, the elegant stone viaduct that carries the Conwy Valley railway over the A470 road and river Lledr south of Betws-y-coed.

## STOKE-ON-TRENT

Leaving Wales, we arrive nearly three hours later at Stoke-on-Trent. I have always been taken by the quality of light and shade through the station roof, probably due to the 220 panes of glass that were restored in 2023.

The 'robust Jacobean manor-house' station buildings were opened on 9 October 1848. The other buildings, including

*(above) Betws-y-Coed Station*

*(opposite) Light coming through the glazed roof on to the platform at Stoke-on-Trent*

*Stoke-on-Trent Station frontage*

the North Stafford Hotel, were opened in June 1849. All were constructed by John Jay (1805–72) to the design of Henry Arthur Hunt (1810–89) at a cost of £31,438. The station was built by the North Staffordshire Railway Company and, until its amalgamation in 1923 into the London, Midland and Scottish Railway under the Railways Act of 1921, housed the company's boardroom and its principal offices.

The Grade II listed building recently had some minor works completed by AHR Group, which also restored the west side of the station that had mainly been used for storage; now it has been altered and fully restored, featuring an original Gothic-style fireplace and areas of autumnal-coloured Minton tiled floors.

## COVENTRY

Fortunately, a direct train sees us arrive at the modern Coventry Station. The Historic England Grade II listing describes it as, 'Outstanding architecturally, particularly for its spatial qualities and detailing'. It replaced a much modified 1838 station, to be reopened on 1 May 1962 in time for a visit by Queen Elizabeth II. The rebuilding was carried out in 1959–62, to designs by Derrick Shorten, with support from John Collins, Mike Edwards and Keith Rawson. Shorten actually visited Denmark and met with the renowned architect and designer Arne Jacobsen, who toured him around several of his buildings for inspiration. Shorten later reminisced that the Head of British Rail instructed him to deliver a new station 'in time for the consecration of the rebuilt Coventry Cathedral' and that 'you are obliged to use the best possible materials ... don't worry about the money'.

Clean, uncluttered, with large light circulation spaces, beautiful detailing and open volumes of modernist staircases and open walkways giving great vistas, it is an iconic station, although possibly not to everyone's tastes. However, my own personal favourite is the materiality, with varnished, warm African hardwood that glistens on the ceiling of the ticket hall. The very tactile handrails and the Genoa marble terrazzo floor reminds me of the similar dark floor at our next station, Euston.

The typefaces around the station are also crisp and beautifully designed (remarkable how much you study something when you are waiting for a delayed train . . .).

The font across the station is in a modified version of the Transport Modern font, created by graphic designers Jock Kinnear and Margaret Calvert, which would later become the standard Rail Alphabet identity, rolled out across the network from 1965.

**EUSTON**

The early morning arrival into Euston is met with the new station hawk whose handler is taking the opportunity of a quiet station to acclimatize the beautiful bird and get it used to its pigeon-scaring duties. It is one of a number of Harris hawks contracted via their handlers by Network Rail to keep pigeons from being a pest to commuters.

There's a lot that could be written about Euston: the demolition of the arch; the booking hall; or the station as a whole and how it encouraged and properly kickstarted the heritage movement. There is, of course, also much to lament, but the truth is more balanced. The old Euston was not the most efficient station and if you look at some of the early architectural renderings, you can imagine how it could have been beguiling to a post-war mentality. Furthermore, if we go back to the nineteenth-century pioneers, as we have seen through all our journeys so far, they had no compunction about flattening the previous station if it no longer suited their needs to build new stations that were bigger and more in keeping with the style of the day. The movement has been inexorably forwards.

The history of Euston is well known. In 1835, Robert Stephenson, chief engineer of the project, gained permission

*(above) Ticket hall and concourse at Coventry Station*

*(top left) Detail of the coat of arms for London & Birmingham Railway*

*(top right) Statue of Britannia that used to preside in the Great Hall at Euston*

*(bottom left) Former Euston Station clock*

*(bottom right) Former Euston Gates*

EUSTON
DEPARTURES
pharmacy
beauty

to build his terminus at Euston Square with a simple train shed and two platforms; one for arrivals and one for departures. Soon after, the grand 'Doric arch' gateway, designed by Philip Hardwick, was built as an impressive entrance to Euston; the station itself opened on 20 July 1837 along with the line as far as Boxmoor. The first inter-city journey from London to Birmingham was made by the directors of the London and Birmingham Railway (this became London & North Western Railway in 1846) on 17 September 1838.

Due to increased rail travel and overcrowding, the station had its first major expansion in 1846, with the new building including the headquarters for the new London & North Western Railway as well as the new entrance to the station, which became known as the 'Great Hall', situated between the Doric arch and the station platforms. At least two more expansions took place before the controversial demolition in 1962.

I can't bring back the old station, but delving through the Science Museum collections brings you back to the old station gates and the original coat of arms that belong to the London & Birmingham Railways. You can also still see the statue of Britannia, which was formerly displayed in the Great Hall of Euston Station over the door leading to the general meeting room from 1849 to 1961, then in the station restaurant from 1962–86. Sculpted by John Thomas in 1849, who also sculpted the lions on the Britannia Bridge, is it now in the National Railway Museum.

We started this journey with a clock and it seems fitting to end it with another – that from the Great Hall at Euston Station, with its black case and gold decoration and gold trim. It stood in the Great Hall of Euston from 1849 until that was demolished in 1963, and it is believed to have been first used on the station platforms from 1837. It is not clear who originally made the clock, but we know it was altered and recased in 1849 for Euston's Great Hall by Thwaites and Reed of London, the great rivals to J. B. Joyce & Co. Thwaites and Reed also made the London & Birmingham Railway Regulator (now in the Science Museum collection). It is a beautiful timepiece, which was used to standardize timekeeping and set watches and clocks along the line.

*Euston Station concourse with the former train indicator board*

JOURNEY

# 8

# MIDLANDS TO THE WELSH BORDERS

## MARYLEBONE *to* HEREFORD

MARYLEBONE

BIRMINGHAM MOOR STREET

BIRMINGHAM NEW STREET SIGNAL BOX

GREAT MALVERN

WORCESTER SHRUB HILL

HEREFORD

Marylebone, London's red-brick gem, epitomizes a mix of Victorian ambition and survival. Conceived by Braddock and Fox as the terminus for the Great Central Railway, it narrowly escaped closure in the 1980s, reborn to serve destinations like Birmingham and Bicester. Further on, Moor Street's early 20th-century charm and Great Malvern's Gothic grace highlight regional styles before Worcester Shrub Hill's Georgian-style facade and intricate Victorian tiles come into view. The journey ends at Hereford, blending Victorian Gothic heritage with modern restoration – a testament to British railway resilience.

MARYLEBONE STATION

## MARYLEBONE

Every time I see the nineteenth-century, red-brick, country house aesthetic of Marylebone, which is in a style otherwise known as Flemish Renaissance, the opening bars of the theme tune to Joan Hickson's *Miss Marple* TV series immediately go through my head. This isn't just because of the episodes' sweeping lines of elegant cars, their designs unfettered by wind tunnel testing, dropping off their passengers with perfectly tailored suits and dresses, clutching their vanity cases with leather trunks at their feet. It's also because two Miss Marple films, *Nemesis* and, ironically, the *4.50 from Paddington*, used the photogenic station as one of their locations. In fact, this beautiful station has a history of doubling up as other railway stations – a bit of an impostor if you like. It starred in The Beatles' *A Hard Day's Night*, masquerading as Liverpool Lime Street (more of that in Journey 2, the TransPennine) and then scans back to Marylebone, this time presumably pretending to be old Euston station!

From Marylebone to Birmingham Moor Street is a leisurely journey taking just shy of two hours. It is then a short walk through Birmingham to its more confident neighbour Birmingham New Street, going past an unsung hero, the Birmingham New Street signal box. Think of the National Theatre-style aesthetic, shrunk and put next to a railway – this building is a listed 1964 Brutalist, verging on cubist, masterpiece without which our journey wouldn't have been possible a few years ago.

*(opposite) Entrance into Marylebone Station*

*(above) Iron and glass porte-cochère between Marylebone and the hotel*

**ELIZABETH BOWEN**
(1899–1973)

Bowen was the author of ten novels, over 100 short stories, one children's book and countless reviews and magazine articles. She was particularly known for *The House in Paris, The Death of the Heart* and *The Heat of the Day*, the latter of which was set in Marylebone. This latter novel has an intense sense of place and time, described through light and movement through the day, which mirrors the two main characters' relationship. Set initially on the fringes of Regent's Park, it moves across Marylebone with evocative descriptions. Towards the end of the novel, the main female protagonist, Stella, is sitting in a train going out of London and looking into the rooms and the houses she passes.

In 1949, when *The Heat of the Day* was published, the railways had recently been nationalised and London and its stations were recovering from the effects of a long war and frequent bombing raids.

*'This is decidedly a novel for the discerning. In probably no other book, incidentally, has the atmosphere of embattled and bomb-scarred London been so perfectly captured.'*

A review of *The Heat of the Day* in the *Belfast Newsletter*, 12 March 1949

*The approach to Marylebone Station*

MARYLEBONE
STATION

*Marylebone Station concourse*

Barely an hour later is Great Malvern's ragstone, French Gothic, 163-year-old station, from which it is a short journey to Worcester Shrub Hill with its rather special waiting room. With its neo-classical look, it is another station that could be mistaken for a country house, if you ignore the less-than-elegant modern office buildings that blight the station forecourt. Once inside, however, it's a different world. Finally, three-quarters of an hour after departing Worcester, we reach Hereford; this time Victorian Gothic in style and having the distinction of being served by a tunnel and viaduct from Ledbury that required five million bricks to build.

Back at Marylebone, a quick trip to Marks & Spencer will let you see traces of the old Victorian ticket hall amongst the shelves – one of many traces of the past.

The station was designed by Henry William Braddock (1859–1929), a civil engineer for the Great Central Railway, and built by the brothers Sir Douglas Fox (1840–1921) and Sir Francis Fox (1844–1927), both engineers. Opened on 15 March 1899 as the London terminus of the Great Central Main Line, it was the last major railway to open in Britain for 100 years and was the last of London's main line termini to be built. It is also one of the smallest, opening with four platforms instead of the original eight planned due to lack of funding.

It is also a great survivor. Its decline initially started in the fifties, the same decade Joan Hickson's *Marple* was set. A decade later, in 1960, all the express services stopped, followed five years later by the freight services, leaving the station eventually only serving Aylesbury and High Wycombe. Irrelevance and decrepitude beckoned and it seemed the final nail in its coffin was about to be struck when a consultation from British Rail in 1984 had the 'bright idea' to turn Marylebone into a 'high speed bus way'.

Fortunately, the idea proved highly unpopular and two years later, amidst much opposition and a legal battle, it was dropped as the scheme was found to be impractical. A reversal of fortunes followed. Rescued in 1986 with an £85-million package, partly funded by selling a portion of the station to developers, less than ten years later it gained services to Birmingham, our first stop on this journey.

Another unique claim to fame is how international Marylebone feels. Where else on the railway network do you get announcements in Mandarin and information posters in Arabic? With a number of bilingual station staff also helping passengers, it may feel quaint and otherwordly in its architecture, but global in outlook. This is of course due to trains going to Bicester Village, the mecca of designer

outlet shopping, as well as Oxford, Leamington Spa and the Bekonscot Model Village.

Next door to the station is the magnificent Landmark Hotel, the original railway hotel, linked by an iron-and-glass porte-cochère to the station. In contrast to the cost-conscious design of the station, it is much more extravagant and boasts Colonel Sir Robert Edis (1839–1927) as its architect, also responsible for the ballroom of Sandringham. It was designed around a vast and completely glazed courtyard, a feature that at the time seems to have been unique in London and provided a dramatic arrival. And the finishing touch? A cycle track on the roof so that businessmen of the day could 'exercise to recover from high living'. With the exception of the cycle track, a number of original features including the glazed courtyard remain, but sadly it doesn't cost three shillings and six pence a night to stay there anymore.

## BIRMINGHAM MOOR STREET

Admittedly, there are quicker ways of getting to Birmingham than going the Chiltern Railways route, but there is something quite sedate about it and other options wouldn't bring you to this wonderful, restored early twentieth-century building that once even hosted a writer-in-residence, quite appropriate for a station that is the start of the Shakespeare Line to Stratford-upon-Avon.

Moor Street, the second-busiest station in Birmingham with five and a half million travellers, is the youngest of our stops and the terminus of Chiltern Railways. It is a merger between the original, which was completed in 1916, and the later addition in 1987. It owes its existence partly to a badly

*(above) Birmigham Moor Street ticket area*

*(opposite) Birmingham Moor Street concourse*

PLATFORM 11

located station. Birmingham Snow Hill was at the wrong end of the tunnel to take traffic from the Stratford-upon-Avon line and so Birmingham Moor Street was built. The two stations were combined in 2002 and fully restored to match the older station in 2010, with a deep clean to ensure it was looking its best for the Commonwealth Games in 2022.

Moor Street was designed not by an architect but by a Great Western Railways engineer, W. Y. Armstrong (1853–1934) and the warehouses by another engineer, Louis Gustave Mouchel (1852–1908), who was the founder of the multi-million-pound UK engineering company Mouchel.

The station-shed architecture is mostly brick and terracotta, with steel and glazed roofs that give a great sense of light to the station and lend a touch of grand regional market hall. My favourite detail is the wonderful original 'Booking Hall' sign in metal above the entrance to the station, picked out with scrolls and gold lettering, though the paint scheme of the station in former Great Western Railway colours are less easy to recreate on a drawing, even if you are colour matching pencils in situ!

## BIRMINGHAM NEW STREET SIGNAL BOX

It's easy to miss this Grade II listed modernist or Brutalist gem. Listed due to its 'dramatic and exceptional architectural quality' and 'strongly sculptural form', it was designed in 1995 by Bicknell and Hamilton, who are known for their transport architecture, especially the Paddington Maintenance Depot (built in 1969, and also

*(above) Birmingham Moor Street café*

*(opposite) Birmigham New Street signal box*

listed). It is overshadowed by its better known, and some would say sexier neighbour, Birmingham New Street Station, rebuilt and redesigned by Foreign Office Architects in 2015. However, this five-storey, nearly sixty-year-old building deserves just as much of a celebration. For me it is the National Theatre of signal boxes.

Two years after its construction in 1966, it started directing trains in the region through the electric power signal box that it contains (as opposed to the older level and frame system), and at its zenith had the capacity to direct up to 1,200 trains a day (nearly a train a minute over a whole day). The Power Signal Box (PSB), to give it its official name, ceased operating on Christmas Eve 2022 after nearly six decades and many millions of trains, although its lower floors are still used by Network Rail. Its critical task, however, has been transferred to the West Midlands Signalling Centre in Saltley, which, while shiny and high-tech in aesthetic, is sadly not as drawable.

Fortunately, this signal box has had a second lease of life and is now used as a training centre, though it is a real shame that the original idea of turning it into a restaurant wasn't entirely feasible.

## GREAT MALVERN

It takes nearly an hour and a quarter to get from Birmingham New Street (a quick walk from Moor Street) to our next stop. Today part of the Cotswold line, Great Malvern was opened by the Worcester & Hereford Railway in 1860, making it nearly forty years older than Marylebone where we first started this journey. When the station and the route opened, the small town of approximately 4,500 people saw a doubling of its population at weekends. Not everyone was amused. In the same year, 1860, the *Malvern Advertiser* reported some 'look on excursionists as a horde of barbarians, whose irruptions [sic] spoil peace, comfort and poetry ... they resent vulgar and noisy people

coming among them.' Just over forty years later another local paper was advertising the charms and attractions of the town and even boasted its 'lowest death rate' in the country!

Now Grade II listed, the station was designed by the architect Edmund Wallace Elmslie (1818–89), who also designed the bridge over the railway, the stationmaster's house and the 'Imperial Hotel' next to the station, now a girls' school.

So, if you were a Victorian staying in the grand spa Gothic hotel next door, how would you stay dry and warm as you went to the station? Well, you'd use the 'Worm', a covered passageway (closed in the seventies) that linked the hotel with the station from the end of Platform 2. With a Romanesque entrance arch, inside it is half-stone, half-corrugated metal roof with windows. It has the feel of an enchanted corridor taking the traveller to a mystical, faraway castle.

Carrying on the fairy-tale theme, Great Malvern's column capitals are some of the most charming amongst British railway stations. Designed by sculptor William Forsyth (1833–1915), the metalwork is a sumptuous array of foliage, flowers and bright colours that wouldn't look out of place propping up a pavilion in the Chelsea Flower Show.

Finally, a mention to Lady Emily Graham (1805–1900), daughter of the 3rd Duke of Montrose (who became Lady Emily Foley after her marriage), with whom I feel a certain sense of affinity. She had the sensibilities of a twentieth-century city planner and thought of garden cities before they had even been envisaged, ensuring Great Malvern was well laid out and had ample green space. When the Worcester & Hereford Railway was due to go across her land, one of her stipulations was the creation of her own private waiting room at Great Malvern.

This exclusive waiting room was transformed into a 'tea room' approximately forty years ago. If all cafés in railway stations were like Lady Foley's Tea Rooms, the world, or at

*(opposite) The former Lady Foley's Tea Rooms*

*(right) Decorated cast-iron column capital at Great Malvern Station*

least the train-travelling world, would be an immeasurably better place. Sadly, the café closed down at the end of October 2023.

## WORCESTER SHRUB HILL

Just over a quarter of an hour later, and we go from one historic waiting room to another at our next stop, Worcester Shrub Hill. Here Platform 2a is the home of the previous ladies' waiting room, which not that long ago was on Historic England's Buildings at Risk Register, but happily is now restored to its former glory, festooned with brightly coloured majolica tiles and burgundy-coloured cast-iron columns.

One of my favourite details in railway architecture has always been the tiles, from the ox-blood tiles of the London Underground to these Victorian, Middle-Eastern inspired tiles by Maw & Company in Worcester Shrub Hill's waiting room. Originally founded in Worcester by George Maw (1832–1912) and his brother Arthur (1834–1911), Maw & Co. even provided tiles for the London Underground (including Piccadilly Circus, Covent Garden and the disused station at Down Street), winning a contract worth £100,000, a substantial sum in the nineteenth century. Their other notable clients included royalty, both British and Russian, the Garrick Club and the Cardiff Library, which still boasts a beautiful tiled corridor.

The rest of this station, built in 1865 and designed by Edward Wilson (1820–77), a locomotive and civil engineer, is more Georgian in character, built using engineering bricks and with an external facade more similar to an austere regional institution than a railway station. Not far away, though, is the rather grander and more impressive Engine Works designed by Thomas Dickson (1812–*c.* 1864) for the Worcester Engine Works Company Limited just a year earlier in 1864. It is a celebration of brick in every way,

*(this page) Maw & Co. tiles in Worcester Shrub Hill*

*(opposite) Elevation of the Worcester Engine Works next to the station*

*Platform 2 at Hereford Station*

with an impressive elevation that spans 125m (410ft) and a central pediment. It is what railway buildings should be – a celebration of transport. It is therefore ironic that the company that commissioned this magnificent edifice sadly went into liquidation only ten years after the construction, partly due to their lavish spending on their company buildings.

## HEREFORD

While geographically sited in England, this station at the end of our journey is actually run by Transport for Wales. Built as one of two stations serving Hereford, and opened in 1856, it is the oldest surviving station structure on our route. Hereford Barrs Court, to give it its original name, was, according to the Grade II listing narrative from Historic England, designed by 'Johnson of Birkenhead'. However, a plaque on the station itself cites John Penson, father of Thomas Mainwaring Penson (T. M. Penson for short), who designed Shrewsbury Station (Journey 6) and, even more intriguingly, Herefordshire Council names T. M. Penson as the architect!

While Marylebone has strong links to Miss Marple, Hereford is linked to another famous detective, Sir Arthur Conan Doyle's Sherlock Holmes, who alights a train in Hereford in the short story, 'Boscombe Valley Mystery' on his way to a jail to ascertain the guilt or innocence of one of the story's main protagonists.

Hereford also has links to the SAS and particularly to Andy McNab's *Bravo Two Zero*, which features scary training regimes and being sent home via the station if you were not deemed fit enough. I had always imagined somewhere quite utilitarian or even spartan, so I was particularly surprised to see the rather bucolic Platform 2 with its cast-iron columns and its slatted woodwork.

Hereford with its gabled facade, octagonal brick chimney stacks and church-like lancet windows is due to benefit from a £20-million facelift, which hopefully means that the windswept car park at the front of the station will be replaced by a beautifully landscaped public space, a new transport hub and, dare I hope, a nice café.

1

JOURNEY 9

# ALONG THE LONDON, MIDLAND & SCOTTISH RAILWAY

## EUSTON *to* CARLISLE

EUSTON

RUNCORN RAILWAY BRIDGE/BRITANNIA BRIDGE

CREWE

PRESTON

GRANGE-OVER-SANDS

CARLISLE

The route from Euston to Carlisle unveils Britain's railway heritage through landmark stations and bridges from Runcorn's fog bell to Preston's red-hued platforms which encapsulate the work of engineers like William Baker. Other stops in the journey such as Grange-over-Sands reflect Victorian tourism, its genteel charm captured in railway posters while Carlisle's Citadel station marks the convergence of railways near the Scottish border, inspiring artists like Réthi and de Grineau to immortalize locomotives not merely as machines but as symbols of progress.

## EUSTON

When looking through the booklet that was produced in 1968 for the opening of the new Euston Station, I was reminded of the power of illustrations to convey an idealized world at a time when colour photography had not quite become mainstream. Railway posters were of course part of this, with their ability to take the would-be traveller to different parts of the country, allowing them to imagine what their holiday or day-trip destinations could be like. In 1939, workers gained a legal right to holiday leave and this, in combination with railway advertising, helped drive an increase in the number of people taking day trips.

It was the excitement of travel that the 1968 booklet was trying to capture. There is a rather alluring illustration of the Euston 'Grill Room', full of very smartly dressed travellers, sadly long gone and replaced with a bewildering array of fast-food joints and sandwich sellers. The concourse also boasted the 'Sprig Buffet' and a licensed bar on the eastern side with waitress service and even a 24-hour 'quick service rail bar'. Finally, the first floor had a fully licensed 'Party Catering Room' seating up to 130 people for banquets and even 'buffet

*(above) One of the Euston Lodges*

*(opposite) First World War memorial at Euston*

**LILI RÉTHI & BRYAN DE GRINEAU**
(1894–1971 & 1883–1957)

Most railway art concentrates on attractive locations, with warm colours that bring you back to the halcyon days of summer. Lili Réthi and Bryan de Grineau, who created posters for the London, Midland & Scottish Railway (LMS), the route of this journey, were different. Lili Réthi, having trained at Vienna's *Kunstschule für Frauen und Mädchen*, became known for her drawings recording German engineering projects between the two World Wars. She escaped to the United States in 1939, where she continued to record major post-War building projects. What sets Réthi apart is that she was interested in construction, locomotive works and sheds rather than the glamour of destinations. Before she emigrated to America, The *Illustrated London News* hired Réthi in 1937 to sketch the coronation of King George VI. While in England, she also created sketches for a booklet issued by the London, North Eastern Railway; posters for the London, Midland & Scottish Railway, particularly the LMS Crewe Works, depicting the construction of a Coronation Class Engine (1937). She also worked extensively for the General Post Office (GPO), the Post Office Motor Transport Depot (1937) and the Post Office Underground Mail Train (1935).

Bryan de Grineau, while not as gritty as Réthi, was also less interested in the destination for his LMS posters than the method and speed of getting there. Born Charles William Grineau on 11 May 1883, he was the son of a well-known illustrator and caricaturist Charles Grineau (1852–99), who used the pseudonym Alfred Bryan, from which Bryan took his own pseudonym and was one of many he used during his professional life (including Phyllis de Grineau when he started drawing flowers). A war artist (during both World Wars), who mainly concentrated on motoring art, nevertheless his posters for LMS entitled 'Travel LMS Speed Comfort' and 'Scot passes Scot' encapsulate the excitement of travel.

dances'. I love the idea that nearly sixty years ago the idea of rail travel was so exciting, you would use the modern, shiny new Euston as a party venue.

The booklet was selling an experience, putting a new train terminus on par with an airport terminal. It was considered somewhere to get to early, spend time in, not just in its restaurants, but also in the hairdressing salon, the gentleman's tailors or the camera shop. While Euston in its current state can't be labelled as a glamorous travelling experience, it does still have some special moments. The single-storey Euston Lodges, built of Portland stone with leaded roofs to designs by London & North Western Railway company engineer and architect J. B. Stansby, are one such moment. Engraved at the corners of the lodges are the names of stations served by the company, while the north and south facades have pediments containing sculptured allegorical figures representing England, Scotland, Ireland and Wales, by Joseph Pitts. The lodges, which flanked the statue of Robert Stephenson by Baron Pietro Carlo Giovanni Battista Marochetti (1805–67), are the only survivors of the formal 1870 layout to Euston Station. The Robert Stephenson statue was moved when the new station was built, and meant to stand in front of the station forecourt, but during the HS2 works was put in storage for safe keeping.

Another moment is the First World War memorial at Euston (1921), designed by sculptor Ambrose Neale (1868–1930) and Reginald Wynn Owen (1876–1950), an architect who worked for the London & North Western Railway. There are three particularly poignant items in the collection of the Science Museum: a typewritten letter to a Mrs Pritchard, who was the widow of Harry Pritchard (a labourer at the

*(opposite) The Ticket Hall at Euston Station*

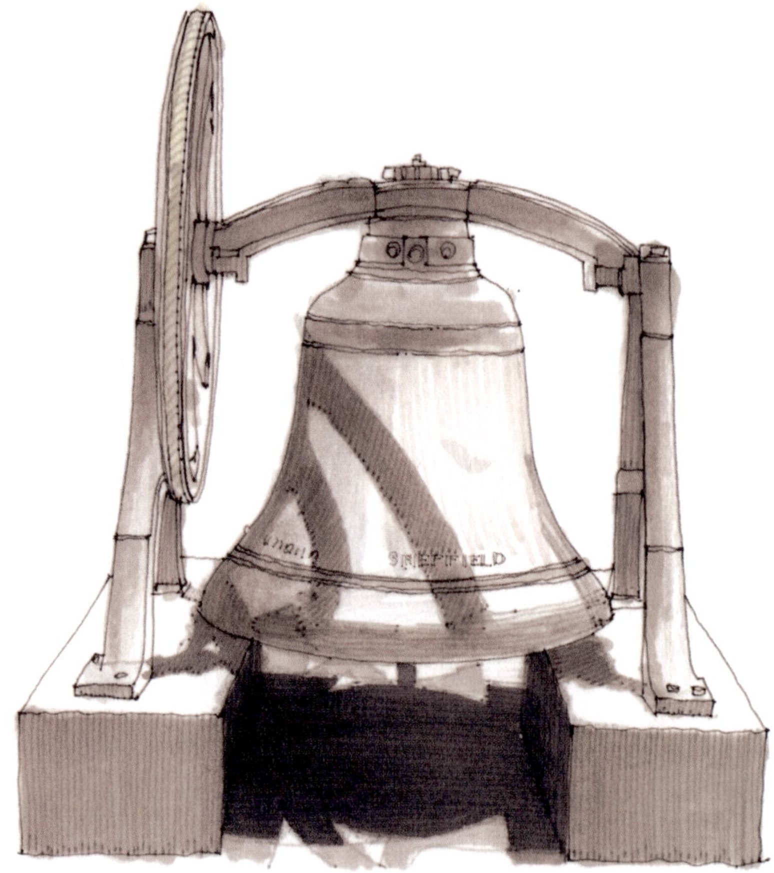

engineering department at Market Harborough, who served as a corporal for the Leicester Regiment 6th Battalion, and died 29 September 1916), inviting her to attend the unveiling of the First World War memorial at Euston on 21 October 1921 by Earl Haig with offers of free travel on the London & North Western Railway – an order of service for the ceremony; and, finally, a paper napkin retained from the luncheon.

Our final moment is the modern travel centre. While some may think it sacrilegious even to mention this in the wake of the demolition of Philip Hardwick's Great Hall, the coffered concrete ceiling designed by R. L. Moorcroft (chief architect for British Rail from 1977) is still rewarding in its mastery of geometry in a quiet dignified, crisp, clean way.

## RUNCORN RAILWAY BRIDGE/BRITANNIA BRIDGE

Two hours on from our tour of Euston is Runcorn, and a few minutes outside the station is the Runcorn Railway Bridge. It is a bridge with many names, having been also called Queen Ethelfleda Viaduct (after Queen Ethelfleda, ruler of the kingdom of Mercia, whose most northerly border was where Runcorn is today), but also the Britannia Bridge.

Grade II* listed and completed in 1868, it was designed by William Baker (1817–78), who was appointed chief engineer of the London & North Western Railway Company after the death of Robert Stephenson. He also led or was involved in the designs of a number of stations along this journey, including Preston and Crewe.

The bridge, which crossed the Runcorn Gap across the River Mersey, was built to join the line from Crewe to Warrington. The medieval castle turrets of the bridge also bear three shields, one with the image of Britannia and a train crossing the bridge behind her in the background (from the railway company crest), The Liver Bird (the Arms of Liverpool) on the Widnes side and, finally, one with a cross of St George and a sword (the Arms of

London) on the Runcorn side. In the nineteenth century, the bridge also had a fog bell as a navigational aide to stop ships hitting the bridge during foggy days. The bell still exists and was recently restored by Network Rail.

## CREWE

A stop and just over 20 minutes away from Runcorn, we arrive at Crewe Station, designed by William Baker and home of Lili Réthi's LMS poster of 'Crewe Works'. An 1837 lithograph print by Arthur Fitzwilliam Tait (1819–1905), published by Bradshaw and Blacklock (who, two years later, in 1839 would publish the first *Bradshaw's Timetable and Railway Guide*), shows a busy platform at the station with some degree of construction still going on – unsurprising given the station opened in the same year.

The first Crewe Station (and the one depicted in the lithograph) was to the north of Nantwich Road, the last main station before the branch to Liverpool Lime Street at Weaver Junction, with the line then going on to Scotland. The station was rebuilt by in 1849 to accommodate increased traffic following the opening of the line to Scotland, and once again in 1867 after the development of longer trains and an expanding network, when the station was completely rebuilt during William Baker's tenure as chief civil engineer for new works of the London & North Western Railway.

Historic England describes the Italianate Grade II listed buildings as 'one of the best pieces of mid-C19 platform architecture designed anywhere on the London & North

*(above) Crewe Station brick details including the 'Greybeards'*

*(opposite) Runcorn Railway Bridge and nineteenth-century fog bell*

Preston
3

*Platform 3, Preston Station*

Western Railway network, and a rare surviving example nationally of buildings of a major junction station of this period'. My own personal favourite parts are the cream and terracotta bricks and decorations, particularly the 'greybeard' keystones above the arches on the platform walls.

Crewe Station was also the first station to have its own adjacent railway hotel: the Crewe Arms Hotel, built in 1838 and still in use, although substantially rebuilt in 1880. The hotel also had a frequent royal visitor. Queen Victoria used to stay overnight en route to Balmoral in the summers, and she even had her own tunnel built between the hotel and the station so that she could get her train in privacy.

The station was due to have nearly £6 billion of investment as part of the route for HS2. At the time of writing the future for the modernization of Crewe is unknown.

## PRESTON

The facade to Preston Station is another French chateau-style frontage, symmetrical, with cream brick and a small clock face in the centre of its slate roof. The train sheds are of cast iron and steel with roofs of glass and corrugated sheet. Inside, a vibrant, festive red-and-green colour scheme with cast-iron columns with rosette and foliage decorations dominates. The footbridges at the entrance end, which cross over the platforms, are of cast and wrought iron, with white-and-red latticed sides and decorated iron balustrading, all adding to the Christmas colour scheme.

Like most railway stations of this date there is also a war memorial. This one, entitled and dedicated to 'The Preston Pals', was designed by John Shaw (b. 1952) and created on a single piece of flawless slate, installed between Platforms 3 and 4 in 2012. It honours the men of the 7th Battalion, the Loyal North Lancashire Regiment, who volunteered to fight in the First World War, most of whose recruits were from Lancashire, Cheshire and Merseyside. More than half of the regiment was killed during the Battle of the Somme.

Today's building dates back to 1880 and was designed by Cooper and Tullis of Preston (active 1859–93), for the London & North Western and the Lancashire & Yorkshire Railway Companies. The company was founded in 1845 by William

*(above) Preston Station entrance*
*(opposite) Grange-over-Sands Station*

Cooper with Alexander and James Tullis. Despite the death of William Cooper in 1859, the business continued under the same name and major contracts followed, including the Harris Library and Museum and Preston Town Hall.

In 1838, when the station was opened by the North Union Railway, the gradient of the slope of the site was so steep that station staff had to occasionally manually push the trains out of the station. Only eight years later, the station was already busy and congested and the first expansion came in 1850 for the new East Lancashire Railway. Each subsequent line was built by a different company. Rivalry often prevented any co-operation over shared facilities, and so almost every railway line into Preston used its own station. It was not until 1900 that all lines in Preston shared a single station, by which time all the companies had been taken over by one or both of just two companies, the London & North Western Railway or the Lancashire & Yorkshire Railway.

## GRANGE-OVER-SANDS

The 40-minute journey takes us through Carnforth, the station made famous by the 1945 David Lean film, *Brief Encounter*, and the often better-known neighbour to Grange-over-Sands.

Before the railways arrived in 1857, this was little more than a small fishing village on the east coast of the Cartmel Peninsula, overlooking Morecambe Bay. It was the railway that changed its fortunes, bringing in an influx of visitors drawn by the warm climate, and became known as the Torquay (Journey 5) of the north.

The station was opened as Grange on 1 September 1857 by the Ulverstone & Lancaster Railway. It was the idea of John Brogden (1798–1869), a Manchester entrepreneur and building contractor (who also built Manchester Victoria Station and the Liverpool to Manchester Railway – Journey 2), who was supported by William Cavendish, the Earl of

Burlington and later, the 7th Duke of Devonshire (1808–91), whose family home of Holker Hall benefitted from the new railway line.

Twenty years later, driven by Victorian tourism, the station was rebuilt by Edward Graham Paley (1823–95) for the Furness Railway. He also designed the station at Cark & Cartmel, Lancaster Cathedral and the Grange Hotel, erected at the same time as the station.

The best words to describe Grange-over-Sands are Victorian, genteel and pretty with its flower arrangements and the five-bay glass canopy on cast-iron columns, which use the same red-and-green colour palette as Preston, while its exterior is limestone rubble with rock-faced sandstone dressings and Westmorland slate roof. The railway posters for LMS reinforce this view: artworks by Frank Ball and Raphael T. Roussel depict the seaside town in the twenties and thirties, like a crossover between the French Riviera and the Lake District, with fashionably dressed men and women promenading under an idealized rose-golden light.

## CARLISLE

Located 13km (8 miles) south of the Scottish border, it's not surprising that six of Britain's leading railways, three English and three Scottish, converged at Carlisle Citadel Station, together with one smaller company on the English side, making seven railways in all and a transport hub of considerable note. Today the station is also one of the termini of the Carlisle to Settle route, dubbed the 'most scenic' in England. LMS railway posters by Norman Wilkinson, amongst others, depicted the dramatic scenery and steam trains speeding through.

Carlisle Station was designed by architect Sir William Tite, who designed the original Fenchurch Street Station (Journey 3) and twenty-three other stations across the

country and therefore had numerous offices including in France, Carlisle and Scotland. Apparently though, Tite rarely visited Carlisle, sending sketches from London for the drawing office to prepare for the contractors. The Carlisle office was closed in early 1848 because of the financial crisis, with Tite in dispute about payments due to him. He later had to go to court in 1851 to recover his professional fees. His design for Carlisle was carried out and is a cross between Tudor and Gothic. Built at a cost of £53,000, the station was constructed between 1846 and 1848. On 10 September 1847, it was officially opened to rail traffic, even though construction was incomplete and only one long through platform with a bay at each end had been finished.

The dispute over money didn't just end, though, with the architect. There are a number of roundels on the facade of the station, placed over three arches; the central roundel bears the royal arms of Queen Victoria flanked by those of the Lancaster & Carlisle and the Caledonian Railways but the outer plaques, intended for the Maryport & Carlisle and the Newcastle & Carlisle, which did not contribute towards the cost of the station's construction, were left blank – no money, no representation!

The Grade II* station has a multi-bay sandstone elevation of two storeys, capped by slate roofs at different levels with an entrance portico supported by five pointed arches with buttresses in between; to the north of the station's portico, located directly between the main entrance and the station offices, is a square clock tower topped with an octagonal lantern. The overall effect is of a well-endowed Russell Group university rather than a railway station.

*(above) Coat of arms and roundels on the facade of Crewe Station*

*(opposite) Train arriving in Crewe Station*

NetworkRail
Improving
Your Railway

Carlisle Station frontage

*'Those who are accustomed to rely on their own motor car for touring may not realise how little they will miss it in Great Britain. The railways come due to remarkably intimate contact with the country, and the landscape views are generally equal to those from the highroad. In addition, travel by rail affords greater comfort and security and a saving of time and money.'*

The Charm of England 'Overseas Edition – 1933' brochure by London, Midland & Scottish Railway, 1933

THE NORTH BRITISH RAILWAY
COMPANY.

JOURNEY

10

# HEADING NORTH: SCOTLAND

## PITLOCHRY *to* GLENFINNAN

PITLOCHRY

EDINBURGH WAVERLEY

GLASGOW CENTRAL

WEMYSS BAY

OBAN (LOST STATION)

FORT WILLIAM (LOST STATION)

GLENFINNAN VIADUCT & GLENFINNAN STATION

James Miller, a prolific architect of Scotland's railways, shaped stations like Glasgow Central and Wemyss Bay, weaving civic grandeur with functional grace. From Pitlochry's book-laden charm to Waverley's iconic glass domes, his creations echo Scotland's spirit. The journey unfolds over the Glenfinnan Viaduct, a testament to McAlpine's innovation, bridging heritage and the modern and famously featured in the *Harry Potter* films when the *Hogwarts Express* 'flies' over its concrete arches. This railway journey unites past and present – showing Scotland's railways are as poetic as its lochs and lore.

**PITLOCHRY**

Our first stop is, for me, one of the most literary stations on the network, as it boasts the Pitlochry Station Bookshop, which is run by volunteers and has raised over £460,000 for charity since opening. The bookshop came into being through the local council's 'Adopt-a-Station' scheme, which asked the public for ideas to revive the empty buildings at Pitlochry Station. Three local women – Priscilla Lorimer, Elizabeth Templeton and Nancy Cameron – responded with a plan to raise money for charity by selling second-hand books.

All Highland mainline services between Perth and Inverness also stop here. It is also a calling point for the Highland Chieftain, one of the longest train journeys in the United Kingdom, covering a distance of 935km (581 miles) and a time of eight hours between King's Cross and Inverness. The longest direct UK train journey was Aberdeen to Penzance, travelling a distance of 1,263km (785 miles), in approximately 13 hours and 20 minutes to complete along thirty-six stops and, while you can still make that journey, a change or two may be necessary.

Back to Pitlochry. Grade A listed, it was opened in 1863 as part of the Inverness & Perth Junction Railway (IPJR). The southbound platform, in a Scottish-Tudor style and designed by Murdoch Paterson (1826–98), was built in 1883 by local firm Stuart Forbes and Jameson at a cost of £504. Paterson was an engineer and architect based in Inverness who was chief engineer of the Highland Railway. Over a decade

*(above) Pitlochry Station*

*(opposite) Pitlochry Station Bookshop*

later, in 1897, the building on the northbound platform was replaced with a more substantial building to the designs of the Highland Railway's next chief engineer, William Roberts (1848–1918).

There is also a rather ornate and special drinking fountain on the platform dating from 1911. It is a cast-iron fountain with a circular dish on a square pedestal, with a heron and flower ornament on top. It was restored in 2013 to its full technicolour glory with gold embellishments (and even a golden lizard) as part of the 150th anniversary of the station courtesy of the Railway Heritage Trust, Perth and Kinross Heritage Trust, and the Heritage Lottery Fund.

### EDINBURGH WAVERLEY

Edinburgh Waverley has the accolade of being the station in Scotland with the largest number of platforms, numbering twenty in total – three more than Glasgow Central.

When the railways came to Edinburgh, there were three railway stations: North Bridge, Granton Station and Canal Street Station. During the late 1860s, the North British Railway – which owned North Bridge – bought and demolished the two stations of its rivals. In 1869, under a plan from James Bell (1844–1935), the chief engineer, the remaining station was expanded west from Waverley Bridge through the North Bridge, with a low, unobtrusive roof profile that didn't impact the city's skyline, to deal with additional trains and passengers.

The extra capacity proved insufficient and in the 1890s the North British Railway and what was now called Waverley Station had to be expanded. The site was substantial – 9.3 hectares (23 acres) in total – making it the largest station in Britain until Waterloo reopened in 1921. Listed Grade A, the design was the work of many people, including: from 1892–1900, W. R. Galbraith (1829–1914), as

*'Faster than fairies, faster than witches,*
*Bridges and houses, hedges and ditches;*
*And charging along like troops in a battle,*
*All through the meadows the horses and cattle:*
*All of the sights of the hill and the plain*
*Fly as thick as driving rain;*
*And ever again, in the wink of an eye,*
*Painted stations whistle by.'*

*From a Railway Carriage* – Robert Louis Stevenson, 1885

*Edinburgh Waverley ticket hall*

consulting engineer and advisor for parliamentary plans and hearings; James Bell, chief engineer to North British Railway responsible for platforms, signalling and permanent way; J. S. Pirie (1860–1943), site engineer; the Cunningham, Blyth and Westland company (called Blyth and Westland from 1893) as principal structural engineers, including the roof; Herbert Waller Raithby (1870–), chief architect, responsible for the booking hall and offices, as well as later additions.

Two of the defining elements of Waverley are the glass roofs. The main part, originally constructed by the Paisley firm of Hanna, Donald and Wilson (which also made the footbridge at Pitlochry Station), is now made of 28,000 panes of glass and covers an area of 5.3 hectares (13 acres), which makes it the size of the site of Windsor Castle. The second glass roof is the dome above the booking hall, and was added in 1897. The dome has always reminded me of being a smaller version of the Art Nouveau Gallery Lafayette roof in Paris, which was built some fifteen years later in 1912. Why buy online when you can drink in the splendour of the Waverley dome with its coffered mahogany ceiling and Corinthian columns? The only thing missing is the old mosaic floor, which is somewhere underneath the current one, although hints of the quality can still be seen in other parts of the station such as the floor of the Wetherspoons pub in the station.

Like all important railway stations of the age, Edinburgh Waverley also had its own hotel. The North British Hotel (now the Balmoral Hotel) was designed through a competition by William Hamilton Beattie (1842–98) who specialized in hotels but also designed the famous Jenners department store in Edinburgh. Beattie died before the station's completion and it was finished after his death by his assistant Andrew Robb Scott (1851–1914) in 1902. The building, listed Grade A, is Scottish Baronial in style and has a prominent clock tower that is 58m (190ft) high. It

*(above) The Balmoral Hotel, Edinburgh*

*(opposite) Mosaic for the North British Railway Company now in the station's Wetherspoons*

has been maintained by the Scottish clockmakers James Ritchie and Son and its subsidiary Smith of Derby since 1902 (which is also the parent company of J. B. Joyce & Co – see Journey 7), although it is always set three minutes fast (except on Hogmanay) to give passengers time to catch their trains! The only exception to this was in 2020, the first year of the Covid pandemic, when it was left three minutes fast, the reason being that 2020 had been such an awful year it would be better for it to finish earlier.

### GLASGOW CENTRAL

Scotland's busiest railway station is also Grade A listed and has over thirty million passengers using it per annum – it had its own documentary in 2019, following the people who were responsible for making the station function. Historically the station has had its fair share of fame too; John F. Kennedy, then only twenty-two, made his first political speech in 1939 in the station hotel at the request of his father, who was US Ambassador to the UK, to the survivors of the passenger liner *Athenia*, which had been torpedoed while it sailed from Glasgow to Montreal. Other famous people who have passed through the station include Queen Elizabeth II, Laurel and Hardy, Brad Pitt and Angelina Jolie, Richard Branson and Robbie Coltrane.

Glasgow Central was first opened in 1879 and extended between 1899 and 1905 – to give thirteen platforms – by James Miller (1860–1947) and Donald Mathieson

*(above) Platforms in Glasgow Central*

*(opposite) Ornate entrance gates to Glasgow Central Station*

CENTRAL STATION

**JAMES MILLER**
(1860–1947)

I thought hard about who I should profile for this journey. There are a lot of popular culture links within it. J. K. Rowling wrote the final part of the *Harry Potter* series in The Balmoral Hotel next door to Edinburgh Waverley, and in the Warner Brother films the *Hogwarts Express* flew over the Glenfinnan Viaduct, propelling a piece of railway infrastructure into the stratospheric halls of fame. Sir Arthur Conan Doyle was also born in Edinburgh and Holmes and Watson were avid train users. The film *Terror by Night* features a case of a diamond being taken to Scotland by train. However, it felt unfair to celebrate fictional characters over a real person who created and designed some of Scotland's important railway heritage.

James Miller (1860–1947) was a Scottish architect, recognized for his civic and commercial buildings in Glasgow and for his Scottish railway stations. Notable among these are the Kelvingrove Exhibition buildings and the American-influenced Union Bank in St Vincent Street. His lengthy career resulted in a wide range of building types including the sumptuous interiors for the RMS *Lusitania*. In 1888, Miller was appointed to the position of architect on the staff of the Caledonian Railway Company and in terms of this journey, he is also known for his designs and extensions to Glasgow Central Station, Wemyss Bay, Glenfinnan and also Fort William. In total he worked on thirty-three stations across Scotland, meaning nearly 10 per cent of all 362 Scottish stations are linked to Miller in some way, shape or form, which alone ought to mean that he should be celebrated as much as Charles Rennie Mackintosh.

*Glazed iron screen at Glasgow Central Station*

(1860–1935), chief engineer for the Caledonian Railway Company, with steel-work by Motherwell Bridge and Engineering Company. The Caledonian Railway Company's colours of green and gold can be seen across the station, from the main entrance in Gordon Street with its porte-cochère, to the beautiful glazed-iron screen at the junction of Hope and Argyle Street, and even on the ornate cast-iron gates.

The roof of the station is glazed partly on flat roof trusses with the more modern extension in the early twentieth century done in more ornate elliptical arched steel girders. Under the roof, inside the station, is the 4.5-m (15-ft) high, four-faced clock, which was installed in 1882 when the concourse was completed, then set in a wooden framework and topped with a lead-covered cupola. It was replaced in 1962, but the new one was unpopular so a copy of the original was put in place in 1992. Underneath the clock on the station concourse are finely detailed timber station offices and shops.

Delving further below the layers of the station, we come across original Victorian platforms that served suburban lines running from west Glasgow into the city and to the east, and vaults similar to St Pancras (Journey 11), which were used to store beer barrels between cast-iron pillars.

## WEMYSS BAY

Just under an hour and thirteen stops later, we arrive at Wemyss Bay. What is really striking about this station is the lightness and curved, flowing lines of this beautiful, glazed half-torus shaped roof, so very different from its facade,

*(above) Wemyss Bay Station*

*(opposite) The former station at Oban, now demolished*

which is more domestic and half Arts and Crafts movement, half stockbroker Tudor. To complete this wonderful mix of styles, just to the right of the station entrance is an Italianate, half-timbered clock tower.

The Greenock to Wemyss Bay railway was opened in 1865 and absorbed by Caledonian Railway in 1893. The current Grade A listed building was built in 1903 (and designed again by James Miller for the Caledonian Railway), and incorporates the Caledonian MacBrayne Ferry terminal connecting the Scottish mainland to the Isle of Bute.

Inside there is a statue of a small boy with a boat, striding towards the ferry terminal, representing the joy of all the summer holiday trips from this station. The little boy was named 'Bobby' and is the creation of the sculptor Angela Hunter (b. 1951). The station also has a small second-hand bookshop and gallery in the empty first-class waiting rooms, which is operated by the Friends of Wemyss Bay Station and is open six days per week, staffed by volunteers. It is supported by ScotRail as part of the 'Adopt a Station' programme, something that would be brilliant to see across the whole British network.

### OBAN (LOST STATION)

The original Oban station was opened on 1 July 1880 by the Callander & Oban Railway, which was later subsumed into the London, Midland & Scottish Railway in 1923. Today, Oban Station is the terminus of one branch of the scenic West Highland Line and also has the Oban ferry terminal next door. with Caledonian MacBrayne ferries sailing daily to islands including Lismore, Mull, Barra and South Uist.

The current station, built in 1985, is a squat yellow brick affair that replaced a rather wonderful and eccentric collection of buildings that were half Swiss-chalet style with two gable ends and half train-shed-warehouse with a clock-

*(previous spread) Glazed roof of Wemyss Bay*

*(above) The former Fort William Station, now demolished*

*(opposite) Glenfinnan Viaduct*

tower picturesquely situated at the east end. These buildings were destroyed in a fire in 1987.

There are several documents about Oban Station in the National Records of Scotland. The two that are particularly of note are the arrangements for the celebration of the centenary of Oban Station in 1980 and then, only seven years later, listed building consent for the demolition of Oban Station by British Railways and arrangements for a public local inquiry. The records also show two key people associated with the designs of the station.

Early drawings from 1866 show the engineers being B. & E. Blyth of Edinburgh, a company that is still going strong today under the name of Blyth & Blyth. They were involved with a number of Scottish railway stations, including Edinburgh Waverley and Glasgow Central stations. Seven years after the practice was set up, Benjamin Blyth's younger brother Edward joined the company in 1854, which is where the Blyth & Blyth company name originated. Drawings from 1879 show John Strain (1845–1931) both as the architect and engineer. He carried out the extension of the Callander & Oban Railway from Dalmally to Oban, including the construction of a harbour at Oban, and in 1877 he was appointed engineer to the Callander & Oban Railway Company. His obituary from the Institution of Civil Engineers, where he became vice president, adds: 'The extension to Oban was notable for the considerable use made of concrete; and Mr. Strain was, in fact, the first to make use of that material on an extensive scale in permanent railway work.'

### FORT WILLIAM (LOST STATION)

Nearly three and a half hours and twelve stops later, we arrive at Fort William. However the station that I'm describing is not the current one, but the older one located in Station Square next to Loch Linnhe, the pier and the bus

station. Opened in August 1894 it is attributed to our railway architect James Miller with engineers Forman & McCall Partnership of James Richardson Forman and David McCall.

The opening ceremony was performed by Marchioness of Tweeddale, Candida Louisa Bartolucci (1858–1925), wife of North British Railway chairman, William Hay, 10th Marquess of Tweeddale. Her portraits can be found in the archive of the National Portrait Gallery, however, one of the most interesting things about her seems to be that she was the muse for Candida in George Bernard Shaw's 1894 play of the same name. He later commented, 'I had no models for Candida. I borrowed her name from an Italian lady I never met: Candida Bartolucci.' It is quite likely that he came across the very same striking portrait by Millais during his days as an art critic.

Old photographs show a red brick fortress-like structure, with a turret at the corner and arched windows to the side elevations. However, there's a much lighter feel to the interior of the entrance hall, with curved lattice girder structures and signs to a tea room and a bookstall, and a glazed train-shed roof beyond.

Sadly, in 1970, British Railways decided to move the station 640m (700 yards) north of its location. Ironically this was to allow the improvements to the A82 to be implemented, and the construction of a bypass in its place. The last train from this station departed on 7 June 1975 and it was demolished shortly after. The current station is a concrete affair with the aesthetic of a petrol station.

## GLENFINNAN VIADUCT & GLENFINNAN STATION

Described by Historic Environment Scotland as the longest concrete viaduct in Scotland, it was opened to trains in 1901 to connect Fort William to Mallaig and cost £18,904 to build in 1897. It was designed by engineers Simpson and Wilson and built by contractors Robert McAlpine and Sons, which is still in operation today. Robert McAlpine (1847–1934), the founder of the firm, was made a baronet in 1918 and had the nickname 'Concrete Bob' for his use of large amounts of concrete – very apt considering the amount of concrete in the viaduct.

The engineers were a partnership between Alexander Simpson (1832–1922) and Walter Stuart Wilson (1850–1926), formed in the 1880s. Simpson is celebrated today outside St Enoch Subway Station concourse, beside the north escalators, for his work as an engineer and then later as chairman of the Glasgow District Subway.

Glenfinnan Viaduct is made up of twenty-one arches spanning 380m (1,000ft) over the River Finnan and is currently under careful restoration, given its Grade A listed status. The work finished in early 2025 and saw engineers assessing the condition and strength of the viaduct and making improvements beneath the track to keep the stone ballast in place.

Aside from its fame in the *Harry Potter* movies, the viaduct is also commemorated on the Bank of Scotland's £10 notes, and there also used to be a myth that said a horse and cart fell inside a pier of the Glenfinnan Viaduct during its construction, in about 1899. In 2001, radar imaging proved there was a grain of truth in the story but that it in fact happened at another McAlpine concrete rail bridge – the nearby Loch nan Uamh Viaduct.

Going over the viaduct to get to our final stop, it takes just over half an hour to arrive at Glenfinnan Station. Designed by James Miller, the whole station complex, including the ticket office and signal box, are designated Grade B by Historic Environment Scotland. Opened in 1901 at the same time as the viaduct it is quite domestic in scale and 'Swiss chalet' in style. The station building and facilities were repaired, restored and upgraded in 1991 and the station interior now functions as a small railway museum. The museum tells the story of this remarkable stretch of railway and focuses on the construction, impact and operation of the extension in the late-nineteenth century. For those who are keen on the full experience, the museum now operates an old sleeping carriage that sleeps ten people and a vintage dining carriage that serves breakfast, lunch and dinner.

*Glenfinnan Station*

JOURNEY

# II

# MIDLANDS TO THE NORTH-EAST

## NEWCASTLE *to* ST PANCRAS

NEWCASTLE

YORK

KNARESBOROUGH SIGNAL BOX & VIADUCT

SHEFFIELD

DERBY

NOTTINGHAM

LEICESTER

ST PANCRAS

This journey weaves through Britain's railway history, driven by the ambition of George Hudson, the 'Railway King'. Starting in Newcastle, where Hudson appointed John Dobson to design its classical station, his vision steered York's rise as a major rail hub. Knaresborough features Hudson's influence in connecting smaller towns, its viaduct a lasting legacy. At Sheffield and Derby, Hudson's Midland Railway expanded England's network, culminating at St Pancras – a neo-Gothic triumph.

*'Of strong and decided Conservative politics, of excellent business habits, and gifted with an almost Herculean frame, he was soon enabled to assume a lead in all matters of interest to his native town.'*

Profile of George Hudson – *Pictorial Times*, July 1847

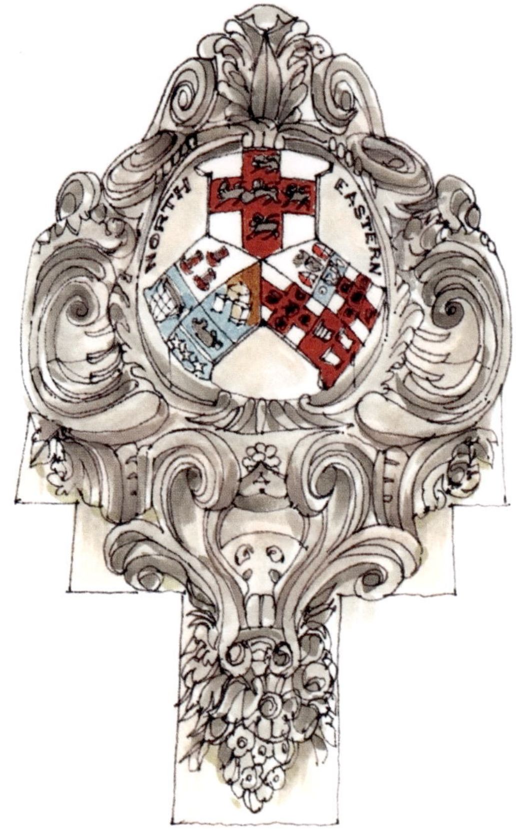


*(right) The coat of arms of the North Eastern Railway at York Station*

*(opposite) Cast-iron column at York Station*

**GEORGE HUDSON**
(1800–71)

A 1991 beer mat made by Webster's Yorkshire Bitter ran a Great Yorkshire Heroes series, featuring George Hudson, the 'Railway King' as number three. Its text reads:

*'At the age of 27, Hudson inherited £30, 000 from a great uncle. (As a result, some said, of bullying the old man on his deathbed.) Lord Mayor of York by the age of 37, Hudson certainly had a nose for business. He boasted that he would 'mak all t'railways come to York' and in the ten years between 1839 and 1849 he increased his railway ownership from 30 to 1,450 miles – quarter of the country's total – earning himself the nickname "Railway King".'*

However, not all heroes are straightforward, not all reputations are completely glowing and one person's hero can be another's scoundrel. This journey and a number of the stations within it, particularly York, becoming a major interchange, were part of Hudson's complex legacy, his empire and the impact he had on the railways and his story.

Born in Howsham, Yorkshire, as the fifth son of a farmer, Hudson became apprenticed to Bell and Nicholson, a draper in York. At the end of his apprenticeship, he received a share in the business and on Bell's retirement, the firm became Nicholson and Hudson. In 1821, he married Elizabeth Nicholson, the daughter of one of the partners.

The inheritance he received from Matthew Bottrill, his great-uncle, allowed Hudson to establish himself and hold a number of key posts, such as that of treasurer of the local Tory party branch in York, at the time of the 1832 Reform Bill; it also served to allow his involvement in setting up the York Union Banking Company, become a councillor in York and, two years later, become Lord Mayor and eventually the MP for Sunderland.

In the mid-1830s he became a friend and then business partner of George Stephenson and learnt about the plans for a railway from London to Newcastle, going through Birmingham, Rugby, Derby and Leeds, but not through York. Hudson managed to persuade a change in direction and in 1836 became the chairman of the newly formed

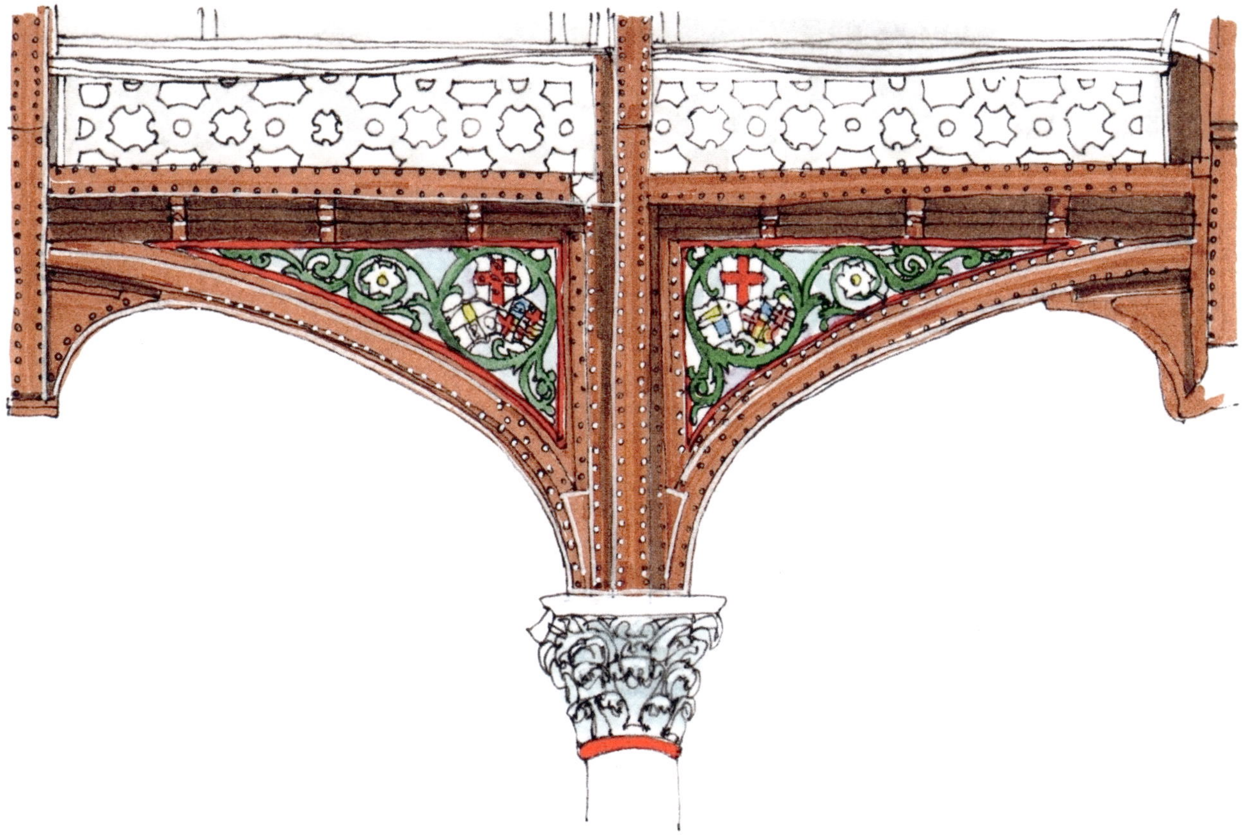

York & North Midland Railway. By 1841, the first permanent station was built in York, changing the city's fortunes.

By the mid-1840s, Hudson controlled over 1,600km (1,000 miles) of railway and was nicknamed the 'Railway King'. His companies controlled over a quarter of the railways then built in England, with lines from Bristol to Newcastle, and branches to Scarborough (which he called 'Brighton of the North'), Hull, Leeds, Nottingham and Rugby, together with the Eastern Counties line. He was not above amalgamating and closing lines that he felt were in direct competition with those he owned.

As the railway mania bubble burst, it became clear that his business dealings were not straightforward: figures of traffic, revenue and expenditure had been manipulated; and there were large sums of money that he was deemed to have misappropriated. He served time in prison and had to sell off his estates and assets to repay some of the debts, although most had to be written off. Intriguingly, his wife and a number of his friends stood by him, lobbying on his behalf and raising a substantial amount of capital from which he could live off the interest.

When Hudson died in 1871 of a heart condition his coffin went through the streets of York, which were lined with mourners and shopkeepers who had closed their businesses out of respect. Obituaries at the time were mixed; overwhelmingly positive, but also with a number of more balanced ones.

Probably the most even-handed of the articles was an earlier piece written by *The Times* in 1849, which stated:

*'But neither the other officials nor the shareholders must hope to escape censure under the cover of a personal onslaught upon Mr. Hudson. The system is to blame. It was a system without rule, without order, without even a definite morality. In 1845 respectable men did monstrous things, and were thought very clever. Thousands rejoiced in premiums which they believed to have been puffed up by mere trickery, collusion, and imposture.'*

In 1849, during the financial scandals, George Hudson Street was renamed Railway Street. In 1971, the centenary of Hudson's death, York City Council decided to rename Railway Street to George Hudson Street once again. The twentieth-century sign for Railway Street was removed and preserved by British Rail.

## NEWCASTLE

Hudson oversaw the early days of the design and construction on Newcastle Station, as part of plans for the line to Edinburgh. He appointed John Dobson (1787–1865) to do the design of the station and Robert Stephenson and Thomas Elliot Harrison (1808–88) on the engineering for the York, Newcastle and Berwick Railway Company, but Hudson's business dealings had caught up with him by the time it was completed in 1850.

Dobson's preferred architectural style was classical and Georgian and this preference is reflected strongly, both in the railway station and in a number of locations across Newcastle, including Grainger Market and Grey Street.

Grade I listed, just as the Newcastle High Level Bridge, the station is constructed of sandstone with a wrought- and cast-iron train shed, supported by cast-iron columns, with a foliage motif at the top of its capitals. Dobson's partiality to Classicism can be seen in the Doric pilasters under the portico at the front of the station and the use of Tuscan-style columns through the station.

The clocks, by Smith of Derby, are a later addition to the station. They came later in 1893, when the entrance portico, or porte-cochère, was built. One clock even went missing, never to be found again (a replica was made), during the construction of the Tyne and Wear Metro, when the portico had to be reconstructed. All three clocks went through restoration in 2024, with new mechanisms installed.

One of the most special spaces in the station is what is known today as the Centurion Bar. Formerly a rather

*(above) Newcastle Station facade*

*(opposite) Centurion Bar and former first-class waiting room at Newcastle Station*

luxurious first-class waiting room, it is a later addition from 1893. It has had a rather intriguing past, though, as it went from well-heeled passengers sipping cups of tea to being acquired by the British Transport Police in the 1960s and used as a collection of prison cells. Fortunately, it was restored in 2000 by its current owners, bringing back to life the beauty of the hand-made Burmantofts (a company that operated from 1859–1957) tiles (also used in the National Liberal Club in London and the Michelin Building). The tiles are now reputedly worth millions.

As we leave Newcastle Station on the way to York, we may catch a glimpse of the High Level Bridge, designed by Robert Stephenson and Thomas Elliot Harrison as the first bridge to carry both road and rail traffic. It was opened by Queen Victoria on 28 September 1849. The public roadway over the bridge was not completed and opened until some six months later. The elegant structure (a tied arch bridge) is made of five masonry piers with its main structural elements made of cast and wrought iron. Today, railway traffic still fully uses the bridge, although the majority of mainline trains use the King Edward VII bridge for reasons of convenience.

### YORK

The station that George Hudson would have known was built by the York & North Midland Railway, outside the city walls, and opened in 1839. Compared to its successors, it was a wooden, temporary and modest affair. Two years later in 1841, it was replaced by what is now 'York old station'. Shortly after the merger of the Y&NMR with Leeds Northern Railway and York Newcastle & Berwick Railway in 1854 to form the North Eastern Railway (NER), it became apparent that the old station was no longer practical and a new station was needed in a better location where through traffic could be facilitated.

*The High Level Bridge, Newcastle*

*Interior view of York Station from the platforms*

The grand station that we all know on this site was opened on 25 June 1877, nearly six years after Hudson's death. Had he been alive to see the new station, I can imagine that he would have been pleased, given that, with thirteen platforms, it was the world's biggest station at the time. It was designed by Thomas Prosser (c.1817–88), architect of the portico at Newcastle Station and the former Immigrant Station and Railway Platform in Hull (Journey 2), and William Peachey (1826–1912), architect of Sunderland and Middlesborough stations.

The design feature that York Station is best known for is its dramatic curve and the vista it creates through the station, necessitated partly by the constraints of the site. The train shed's roof, which was inspired by Paddington Station and Crystal Palace, is supported by cast-iron columns and wrought-iron trusses that bear the coat-of-arms of North Eastern Railway, lest anyone should forget the railway company that had built such a magnificent station. Today's roof structure is a slightly simplified version of the original, which was, sadly, badly damaged during bombing in the Second World War.

Next door to the station is what will hopefully in the future be York Central, a regeneration on the scale of the railway lands of King's Cross, delivering new homes, retail, offices and an extension to the wonderful National Railway Museum, home to the *Mallard,* and *Locomotion No. 1*, which is on display at its Shildon site (Journey 1).

York remains a key interchange, and services are currently run by London North Eastern Railway, CrossCountry, East Midlands Railway, TransPennine Express, Grand Central and Northern Trains.

### KNARESBOROUGH SIGNAL BOX & VIADUCT

Less than 30 minutes later, we're at Knaresborough Station.

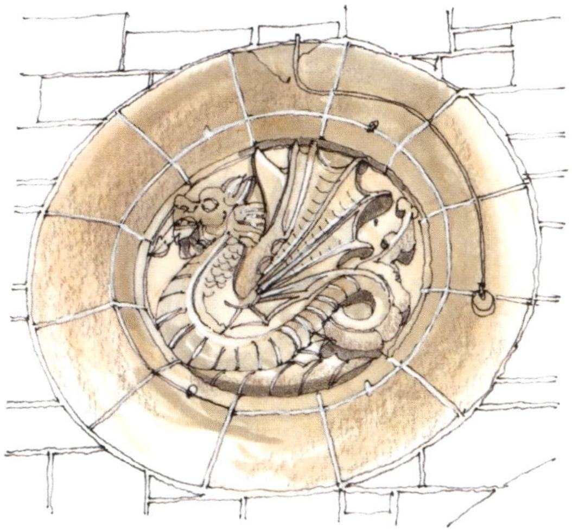

*(above) Griffin roundel on the facade of Sheffield Station*

*(right) Knaresborough Viaduct*

*(opposite) Knaresborough Signal Box*

What is particularly unusual about the station is actually its signal box. It's not freestanding but attached to a row of terraced houses, like a small semi-detached home. The level crossing that is linked to the signal box is also still manually operated with a twelve-lever McKenzie & Holland frame.

It is Grade II listed and opened in 1872, with possible alteration in 1890. Two storeys and only one bay wide, it is made of a type of hard, coarse-grained sandstone called gritstone, with a grey slate roof. On the top floor there is an eighteen-pane sash window giving a clear view up and down the track.

The viaduct that we will go over shortly was built in 1851 by Thomas Grainger (1794–1852) for the Leeds & Thirsk Railway to carry the Harrogate line. Grainger was very experienced in railway bridges, viaducts and tunnels and was actually brought in as an arbitrator when the original viaduct collapsed. Work started on the construction in 1847, but it subsided into the river a year later, with a 'tremendous crash' when it was very near to completion. There was never a full inquiry but the collapse was seemingly due to a variety of factors, including excess rainfall over a two-month period leading to a swollen river, as was reported in the *Evening Standard* at the time, and bad workmanship. The reports in the *York Herald*, of the completion of the viaduct, remark slightly caustically that it 'now appears, to stand permanently'.

Grade II* listed and again made of gritstone similar to our signal box, it is approximately 100m (330ft) long and 30m (100ft) high, carrying two tracks on four arches, with two arches spanning the River Nidd. The top is castellated and, in keeping with the medieval character of the viaduct, there are fake arrow slit windows on each of the columns. In 2015, the viaduct was voted into the top fifty views in Yorkshire.

**SHEFFIELD**

Sheffield Station used to be known as Pond Street Station and then Sheffield Midland. It was the terminus of the new route to London of the Midland Railway Company, one of the largest and most influential railway companies of the railway era. The station marked the successful completion of the company's direct line from Sheffield to London and was the largest station complex on its network apart from St. Pancras Station in London.

The original 1850s building was designed by John Holloway Sanders (1825–84), who at the time was the Midland Railway architect. The station we know today (Grade II listed) opened in 1904, the work of Charles Trubshaw, who was also the architect of a number of stations in this journey.

I have always been particularly taken with the warm, sandy, honey masonry of the station facade with its engravings of mythical creatures, bearing the wyvern crest of the Midland Railway Company, offset by a much-improved public realm and a modern, striking water feature. The water sculpture in Sheaf Square outside Sheffield Station is a homage to the city's steel manufacturing past. Called Cutting Edge, it is a stainless-steel sculpture enveloped with a waterfall that is 5m (16ft) high and goes on for 90m (300ft). The feature was designed by the Sheffield design team Si Applied and international glass artist Keiko Mukaide.

Just like Newcastle Station, Sheffield also has a restored pub, called the Sheffield Tap, in what used to be the station's first-class Edwardian refreshment and dining rooms. With grants from the Railway Heritage Trust as well as private investment, decades of disuse and abuse were turned around from 2008. The incredibly ornate plaster ceiling is a handmade replica that had to be taken from the original moulds. The old mahogany bar was also rescued from the

original so that it could be returned to its original home. The walls of this pub are worth more than a second look as they are covered with ornate, intricate cream-white tiles. It is obviously a great space to spend at least a few minutes, or even longer for a drink or two if your train is delayed!

Befitting its status as the world's pre-eminent steelmaking and manufacturing centre in the late-nineteenth and early-twentieth century, the station is home to both CrossCountry and East Midlands Railway services to destinations such as Reading, Newcastle, Cardiff, Nottingham, Crewe and Derby.

## DERBY

Francis Thompson (Journeys 7 and 14) was the architect for the old Derby Station, which we sadly can see very little trace of today. It must have been something really quite special, with some calling it 'admirably contrived and elegant' with 'spacious platforms' and others as 'the most complete structure of the kind in the United Kingdom or perhaps the world'.

At Derby Station it seems Thompson created one of the first complete railway complexes. He designed not only the station building and the train shed, but he also added workers' housing, a railway workshop, a magnificent hotel that still survives, and a locomotive roundhouse.

The Derby Roundhouse, which was actually the world's first railway roundhouse, jointly designed by Robert Stephenson and Thompson in 1839, is today a Grade II listed building, which has been restored and is now used as part of Derby College. It is a magnificent structure designed as a

*(above) Sheffield Station's pub, the Sheffield Tap*

*(opposite) Exterior of Sheffield Station looking over the water feature*

*The old Derby Station, now demolished*

DEPARTURE
CARRIAGE-ENTRANCE

*(left) The interior of the Derby Roundhouse*

*(opposite) Carrington Street entrance to Nottingham Station*

polygon of sixteen sides and it would have had a turntable, so that when trains arrived the engines would be taken here, placed on it and wheeled into an empty stall.

Later commentators, such as Caroll Meeks a century later, were also appreciative, noting:

*'the central motive is a pavilion with an arched recess flaming the main entrance ... Once established the motive is repeated at intervals and in diminishing sizes sometimes with the doors sometimes witnesses the round headed motive was repeated along the sides of the trainshed in spite of the unity and simplicity of the scheme however nothing could mitigate the fact that though the facade was 1,050 feet long it was only 40 feet high.'*

So, while clearly liking the train station, he was not completely enamoured with its proportions!

The traces of Derby Station that remain, such as the hotel and the workers' housing, are augmented by a series of engravings in the Science Museum collection showing the interior of the early station (not the Victorian expansion) as an airy, light and well-proportioned train shed with platforms. To me, some of the most exciting of these engravings are those of the exterior of the station: there is one in particular that looks to be hand-coloured, with a cow walking casually in front of the grand classical portico and facade of the station, which gives you an idea of its scale in 1851.

It is also not surprising that the 'Railway King' himself, George Hudson, was involved in getting the Midland Railway Company to build a line through Derby in the 1840s. The station is also notable as it is where the first sketch of what would become Crystal Palace was drawn. Joseph Paxton, a director of the Midland Railway Company, drew the building at a board meeting held at the station in 1850.

The Victorian station that is illustrated here was designed by Charles Trubshaw and was sadly demolished as late as

1985. Its pavilions, corner turret and cupola can now only be seen in photographs and drawings.

### NOTTINGHAM

The original Nottingham Station, built in 1839, is now a magistrate's court and today's Grade II* listed station is on the opposite side of the road. Built for the Midland Railway in 1904, what is really striking about the station is the use of red brick and terracotta across the whole facade and interiors, giving it presence even on the greyest, wettest days.

Externally, the baroque detailing in the columns, doorways and pediments are set off with polychromatic banding and intriguingly art nouveau wrought-iron gates. Inside, the station is spacious, helped by the glazed roofs and further polychromatic banding that carries your eye across the spaces. The terracotta detailing is magnificent, especially in the pediment above the Co-op, which has the initials of the railway 'MR' intertwined amongst acanthus leaves. The ticket hall, a vast, handsome space with glazed tiling and herringbone parquet floor, is crying out for an alternative use beyond the greeting of the rail company mascot. Clearly, none of this came cheap, even over a century ago, costing £1 million to ensure it was keeping up with rival stations that have since closed.

A plaque inside the station heralds the architects and reads: *'Constructed by the Midland Railway to designs in the Neo-Baroque style by company architect Charles Trubshaw, with external detail by local architect Albert Edward Lambert, and opened in January 1904. The station is Grade II* listed. Major refurbishment of the station took place in 2014 in conjunction with the extension of the Nottingham tram system.'*

Albert Edward Lambert (1869–1929) was a local architect who also designed Nottingham Victoria Station (now demolished) and a large number of buildings across Nottingham, including many churches that can still be seen today. Charles Trubshaw (1840–1917) as chief architect to the Midlands Railway Company was responsible for many Midland Railway stations, including Leicester, Skipton and Derby, and the Midland Hotel in Manchester, well into the first decade of the twentieth century.

*(below) Terracotta pediment above the Co-op in Nottingham Station with the letters 'MR'*

*(opposite) The terracotta tiled departure gateway at Leicester Station*

### LEICESTER

Only one stop away by the fastest direct train, both Nottingham and Leicester have a strong similarity in architectural styles, both neo-baroque in feel and with the same polychromatic banding with red brick and terracotta detailing. Not surprising, given the later station that we see today was also designed by Trubshaw and built between 1892–95 (although only Grade II listed). The only things to survive from the earlier, much more classical-looking station (think Huddersfield), which was opened in May 1840 (and which Hudson would have recognized from when he was chairman), are a pair of stone gateposts just beyond Campbell Street in the car park.

The station also has three other interesting features: the arrival and departure gateways with the signage in terracotta tiling above so that coach and cab drivers knew where to pick up and drop off passengers coming to and leaving the station; the clock on the station frontage, which is the only remaining hand-wound station clock in Britain; and finally, just outside the station, is the statue of Thomas Cook, who used the original Campbell Street Station for some of his first organized excursions.

Leicester is now served by CrossCountry and the East Midlands Railway and it is the latter service that will take us to our final stop at St Pancras.

### ST PANCRAS

I first visited St Pancras Chambers in 1995 as part of a recent initiative called Open House, which allowed the public to view and appreciate buildings that were usually not accessible. It had been left empty and semi-derelict for a decade. But Sir George Gilbert Scott's incredible architecture with the remnants of the Victorian glory days of railway travel were still evident in the building.

Of course, there was also St Pancras Station next door and, while not in the same state as Saint Pancras Chambers next door, as a station it was looking tired and was confusing to navigate. What really brought on the regeneration and rejuvenation of these buildings was a transport project – Eurotunnel to be exact. But what really saved them at the

*(left) Exterior, Leicester Station*

*(opposite) St Pancras Renaissance Hotel from the Euston Road*

very outset was the destruction of Euston, which started the heritage preservation movement. St Pancras had been badly damaged in both World Wars and there were also plans in the 1960s to demolish it and divert trains elsewhere. There was a hard-fought and passionate campaign to save the building, led by Jane Fawcett (1921–2016), the poet Sir John Betjeman and the Victorian Society. Fortunately for us, this ultimately succeeded and with ten days before the station was due to be destroyed, in 1967, it was awarded Grade I listing status, one of only a handful of stations to achieve this.

Let us go back in history to find out how this magnificent collection of buildings evolved. We have already spoken a lot about the Midland Railway and its ambitions. It became clear in the mid-nineteenth century that it needed a terminus in London that had capacity for the increase in rail travel.

The station was designed by William Henry Barlow (1812–1902). Barlow was an engineer by profession and worked initially for the Midlands Railway and then formed his own consultant engineering practice. He was not only involved in the design of St Pancras, but also supported Paxton in the structural calculations for Crystal Palace and completed the Clifton Suspension Bridge following Brunel's death.

In 1866, the construction on St Pancras Station began and two years later it was completed, with work then starting on next-door's hotel, designed by Sir George Gilbert Scott, and opened in 1873. St Pancras has gone through many changes since its construction approximately 150 years ago, but the most significant was its transformation into the Eurostar terminal in 2007. The work was done by London and Continental Railways in partnership with the engineering companies Bechtel, Halcrow, Arup and Systra. The masterplan of the new complex was created by Foster & Partners but the original reference design was done by Nick Derbyshire (1944–2016), who was former head of British

BUS
LANE

Rail's architecture team, with Alastair Lansley (1947–present) as the lead architect of the reconstruction. In 2011 the former St Pancras Chambers reopened as a new hotel and apartments.

The restoration work was painstaking – part of the station was rebuilt using sixteen million bricks that had to be made exactly like the originals. The train shed had 18,000 panes of glass changed and restored alongside 300,000 pieces of Welsh slate. The iron roof supports were also restored to the original pale blue colour. The overall feel of the station is much more open, spacious and airy, not forgetting all the extra facilities such as shops and restaurants that have also been put into the station.

Just before we leave, there is time for two other stories: one is about the public, but the other is about the clocks.

*I want my time with you* (2018) by Tracey Emin (b.1963), is a statement in her handwriting in neon lighting beneath the dent clock. It is very much about arrivals, departures and being met by loved ones at a station platform. The other highlight is the statue of the poet Sir John Betjeman, one of the key people who campaigned to save the station. The larger-than-life sculpture, at well over 2-m (6.5-ft) tall, was done by Martin Jennings (b.1957).

No station is complete without a clock. As part of the restoration works at St Pancras Station, there was a desire to bring back the Dent clock that now sits above Tracey Emin's artwork. The issue was that no one quite knew what had happened to it. The story went that it had been sold for a considerable sum of money to an American, but no records remained and it eventually came to light that when the clock was being taken down, it was dropped and shattered. As the story unfolded, a train guard had paid £25 for it, taken its pieces and rebuilt the clock. While the original could not now be used it was taken as a template to build a new Dent clock, exactly the same as the original, on the far wall of the station.

*St Pancras Station interior, looking down into the shopping area*

Underground
St.Pancras

JOURNEY

# 12

# SEASIDE TRAVELS

## LONDON VICTORIA *to* LONDON BRIDGE

LONDON VICTORIA

OUSE VALLEY VIADUCT

LEWES

EASTBOURNE

RAMSGATE & MARGATE

LONDON BRIDGE

Beginning at London Victoria, a testament to Edwardian grandeur with redbrick and white stone facades, once a hub for glamorous travel to Europe, containing the platform memorial to the Unknown Warrior, this journey highlights the architectural evolution of Southern Railway's coastal gems. The Ouse Valley Viaduct with its 37 Italianate arches, designed by David Mocatta and John Rastrick, blending Caen limestone and redbrick. Lewes offers a single-storey Gothic station with elegant cast-iron detailing, while Eastbourne channels French chateau influences. Concluding at Ramsgate and Margate where modernist architecture met booming seaside tourism in the 1930s, crafted by the modernist Edwin Maxwell Fry.

**LONDON VICTORIA**

Victoria has long been linked to glamorous travel. Trains to the French Riviera, the *Orient Express*, the *Night Ferry* to France and Belgium, as well as the more domestic *Brighton Belle*, have cemented that look of the traveller with the perfect cashmere twinset and pearls, with perhaps a Louis Vuitton trunk being wheeled behind her by a station guard as the sound of her heels reverberated on the station floor.

Once upon a time it was even possible to take the boat plane from Victoria, travelling from the Imperial Airways Empire Terminal, which was opened to the public just before the onset of the Second World War in 1939. It was part of a truly integrated transport system and Albert Lakeman (1883–1969), its architect, described it as 'the finest air terminal in the world'. Nestled between London Victoria Railway Station and Victoria Coach Station, at 157–197 Buckingham Palace Road, today the building is amusingly home to the National Audit Office, not known for either glamour or luxury. Above the building, you can still see the sculpture *Wings Over the World*, designed by Eric Broadbent (1896–1965). It is the only clue that remains of what the building was once used for. In its heyday, it had direct access to what is now Platform 19 of London Victoria. If you were that woman with a twin set and pearls and Louis Vuitton trunk, you would be welcomed on a special train made up of first-class Pullman carriages to take you to the flying boat service from Southampton. The link with international travel remains with the Gatwick Express service, which was introduced in 1984, all very much in keeping with Ernest Bevin's quote.

With the exoticism of foreign travel, it's no wonder that Victoria Station is also a literary staple. It features in Henry Green's 1939 novel *Party Going* about a group travelling to the French Riviera, and again in Cecil Roberts' novel *Victoria Four-Thirty*, also set in the late 1930s, about thirteen different

*'My policy is to be able to take a ticket at Victoria station and go anywhere I damn well please!'*

Ernest Bevin's definition of his foreign policy. Attributed to Bevin in *The Spectator*, 20 April 1951

characters and their motivations, travelling to continental Europe via the 4.30 train from Victoria. Other literary links include Oscar Wilde's *The Importance of being Ernest*. Ernest Worthing, as we find out during the course of the play, was actually left as a baby in a black handbag in Victoria Station and given the name 'Worthing' as the finder had a first-class ticket for Worthing in his pocket. There are parallels here to Fenchurch, from *The Hitchhiker's Guide to the Galaxy*, who came into being as a result of a ticket queue at Fenchurch Station (Journey 3). Railway stations will always play an important role in our imaginations.

So how did Victoria Station come into being? In the mid-nineteenth century there was fierce competition to bring railway lines into the West End of London. Two railway companies, the London Chatham & Dover Railway and the London Brighton & South Coast Railway, came to the conclusion that it was better to pool their resources rather than compete and together they backed Victoria Station and Pimlico Railway, which had been given the authority to create a western terminus. They had bought 5.7 hectares (14 acres) of land on the spot where Victoria Station now stands. The only issue was that this still led to the creation of two stations: one by the architect Sir John Fowler (1817–98); the other by the engineer for the London and Brighton Railway, Robert Jacomb-Hood (1822–1900). The London Brighton & South Coast Railway's segment was first to be finished, in 1860, with the London Chatham & Dover Railway's section completed two years later in 1862. However, this is not the

*(opposite) Guards band playing at Victoria Station*

*(above) Platform 8 at Victoria Station with its plaque to the Unknown Warrior*

SOUTHERN
RAILWAY
London Victoria Station
BIGBUS.COM
MTG
LT7AS

*Victoria Station and bus interchange*

station we see today. The 1860s buildings were really no more than temporary wooden structures. Finally in 1899, the London Brighton & South Coast Railway bought the Grosvenor Hotel and designed a frontage by their chief engineer Sir Charles Morgan (1792–1875) to link into it. It was quite a flamboyant and almost continental European-meets-Edwardian style in red brick and white stone. The station, or at least this side of it, was completed in 1908.

Meanwhile, the rival railway company, seeing what the other side were up to, commissioned the architect Arthur William Blomfield (1829–99), responsible for the Royal College of Music and many churches, to remodel their half of the station. Theirs, however, was in white Portland stone to show that it belonged to a different company. Finally, in 1923, both railways were merged into the Southern Railway, when two stations finally became one.

The station today is part railway terminus part 1980s-inspired shopping centre. However, it does retain some wonderful features. Just outside the station, there is 'Little Ben', the mini Victoria clock tower. The clock was commissioned by the vestry of Saint George's Hanover Square and sits right next to the public lavatory. Its position at the junction of Victoria Street on Vauxhall Bridge Road was because people hurrying for trains would not at that point be able to see the time on the face of its big brother. Built by Gillett and Johnston, it was unveiled in 1892.

There is a wonderful rhyme towards the base of the clock tower which says:

*My hands you may retard or may advance*
*My heart beat true for England as for France*

The short poem refers to the clock being permanently on daylight saving time so as to be correct for the UK during the summer and right for France during the winter months, when passengers would catch the boat train from Victoria Station. However, when the clock was restored by Smith of Derby in 2016 this charming gesture towards Anglo-French timekeeping was not kept and now it only keeps UK time.

Two more quick things to look at before we go to the Ouse Valley Viaduct. The first, as we enter Victoria Station, are the two special mosaic maps. One shows the roots of the London Brighton & South Coast railway, the other the map of suburban lines, most of which are the same today. Look closely at the bottom of the system map and you can even see a little ferry making its way to France across the English Channel.

Finally, before we leave, a short pause at Platform 8. This is a part of the station not many people visit, unless they're catching a train from it. Here, you have a unique memorial.

The body of the British Unknown Warrior arrived at Platform 8 at 8.32 p.m. on 10 November 1920 and lay here overnight before internment at Westminster Abbey on 11 November 1920.

To this day the Western Front Association hosts a public annual commemoration event to remember the arrival of the body of the Unknown Warrior, which takes place on 10 November at 8.00 p.m.

## OUSE VALLEY VIADUCT

Lauded as 'One of England's most impressive railway viaducts', eleven million bricks went into the building of this magnificent Grade II listed structure. designed by David Mocatta (1806–82), architect, and with John Urpeth Rastrick (1780–1856) as the engineer.

Mocatta studied under Sir John Soane and designed balustrades and a set of eight Italianate pavilions to ornament the Ouse Valley Viaduct and was also the architect of Brighton Station as well as a number of other railway stations, including East Croydon and Haywards Heath. Rastrick was what we would recognize as a mechanical engineer by trade, having been an apprentice to his father at the Ketley ironworks. He had his own company, Bradley, Foster, Rastrick & Co., ironfounders and manufacturers of machinery at Stourbridge. He was also a judge at the Rainhill Trials (Journey 1), where Stephenson's *Rocket* was triumphant. Rastrick also had other links with Stephenson and worked with him in surveying the line from Birmingham to join the Liverpool & Manchester Railway.

Opened in 1842, the Ouse Valley, or Balcombe Viaduct, as it is also known locally, is 29m (95ft) tall, and has thrity-seven arches, stretching 450m (1,475ft) across the Ouse Valley and over the River Ouse. It is built of red brick and Caen limestone from Normandy and cost £38,500. What is unusual about the viaduct is the closing of the arch at the bottom of each pier. This is designed to spread the load. Network Rail

*Looking through the brick arches of the Ouse Valley Viaduct*

has just completed an eighteen-month restoration project on the viaduct.

Today, the Ouse Valley Viaduct still connects Brighton and London and carries nearly seventeen million passenger journeys every year.

## LEWES

Once over the viaduct, it's only about 24km (15 miles) to Lewes. The current station, built in 1889, which replaced one from 1846, was described by the Victorian press as:

*'The building is in Gothic style, and its architectural features have a very pleasing effect. Mr Henry Davey, of Lewes, and Mr Fabian, of Brighton, are the builders.'*

I would describe the Grade II listed station more in the style of an Italian pavilion although Historic England has a different opinion altogether and goes for 'flamboyant classical' in its listing. Overall it has a genteel seaside aesthetic rather at odds with the films that feature it, such as *Corruption* (1968), which focuses on a series of murders, and Eddie Izzard and John Hanna' s *Circus* (2000), a gritty, urban crime-fuelled drama.

Designed by Rastrick and built of stock brick with red brick and stone semi-circular arches, it is single storey and has a wooden canopy at the front supported by two cast-iron columns. The parapet round the top of the building has wonderful detailing of acorns with spikes protruding from the top. At the centre of the roof is a large central rectangular lantern, bringing light to the ticket hall.

Equally importantly, Lewes is part of a handful of stations, like Pitlochry and Wemyss Bay (Journey 10), that has a bookshop. It is aptly named 'The Station Bookshop'.

## EASTBOURNE

Like a number of our stations, Eastbourne has been built and rebuilt several times. In this case, the present building is its third incarnation, with nearly forty years between it and the first (1849–86).

There are definite parallels between the design of Lewes and Eastbourne. Both are Grade II listed, built of stock brick

*(top) Lewes Station exterior*

*(bottom) Eastbourne Station exterior*

Except buses
at any time

**SOUTHERN RAILWAY**
(1923–48)

The 1921 Railways Act was an Act of Parliament to stop the losses being suffered by the 120 railway companies that existed across the company. The Act grouped them into four large companies, known as the 'Big Four', one of which was the Southern Railway, formed by bringing together several smaller railway companies, the largest of which were the London and South Western Railway, London & Greenwich Railway, London Brighton & South Coast Railway and South Eastern & Chatham Railway (a working union between London Chatham and Dover Railway and the South Eastern Railway).

The Southern Railway had control over all the stations in this journey and four other London termini: Blackfriars, Cannon Street, Charing Cross and Holborn Viaduct (as well as Victoria and London Bridge on our route). Even so it was the smallest of the big railway companies, with a route mileage of 3,518km (2,186 miles).

Even during its short period of operation before it was nationalized in 1948 to become the Southern Region of British Railways, it achieved a number of important firsts, such as being the only main-line railway to fully embrace electrification, becoming the operator of the world's largest electrified suburban network. This encouragement of modernity can also be seen reflected in their stations such as Surbiton, Ramsgate, Margate, Richmond and Malden Manor.

They were also the only real way to use passenger ferries, with services such as the Golden Arrow, which had its own channel ferry between London and Paris. Finally, operations into the continent did not stop with normal passengers. The Southern Railway had a critical role in Operation Overlord in 1944, in embarking the British military during Dunkirk.

*The glazed canopy inside Eastbourne Station*

with similar red brick and stone-arch decorations around their windows, with lanterns on their roofs. Eastbourne though, is more confident, more lavish. Everything is bigger; part rural French chateau with Italian, classical influences. It has a dome and a prominent clock tower that announces itself with the coat of arms of the London Brighton & South Coast Railway directly beneath it. Probably rather befitting for a seaside town that was originally laid out by its landowner, the Duke of Devonshire.

The 1886, the station was rebuilt to designs by F. D. Banister (1823–97), chief engineer to the London Brighton and South Coast Railway, who considered himself both and engineer and an architect and had a love of Italian architecture. Today, his personal copies of various architectural drawings of the buildings he designed for the London Brighton & South Coast Railway are held by RIBA.

*(above) Margate Station*
*(opposite) Ramsgate Station interior*

### RAMSGATE & MARGATE

Only eleven minutes and two stops separate these two stations, but both of them transformed and boosted tourism to their respective seaside resorts.

Their architectural styles are also very close. It originally consisted of three stations (Ramsgate, Margate and the now demolished Dumpton Park) with a similar architectural aesthetic, which Edwin Maxwell Fry (1899–1987) designed when he joined the architect's department of the Southern Railway in 1924 as its chief assistant to James Robb Scott, the company's chief architect.

Both stations (Grade II listed) reflect Fry's classical training under Charles Reilly at the Liverpool School of

Architecture and the influence of Charles Voysey. As one of this country's foremost modernist architects, he did not discuss his railway work as much. This is a shame, as the stations clearly show that stepping stone between the Edwardian architecture of the earlier stations at the turn of the twentieth century, such as Victoria at the beginning of this journey, and the modernist Surbiton (Journey 13).

The use of semi-circular windows, brick facades and imposing elliptical booking halls with their painted line borders and pendant lighting are clearly of the same architectural language and highlight the idea of a grand station in a new architectural style.

In the 1930s, Fry embraced modernism, designing the well-known Kensal House flats (1937). He even worked in partnership with Walter Gropius on projects including apartments in St Leonard's Hill, Windsor (1935); Impington Village College in Cambridgeshire (1936); and Levy House in Chelsea, London (1936). Other partnerships included Le Corbusier, with whom he collaborated on Chandigarh.

## LONDON BRIDGE

London Bridge, the most recent of the London termini to be regenerated and partly rebuilt, underwent a five-year, £1bn redevelopment, completed in 2018, to help meet the transport demands of the future. For the first time, a large concourse now unifies the station and gives step-free access to every platform. Designed by the firm Grimshaw, the wooden slats that travel horizontally across the ceiling of the concourse give a warmer feel to an otherwise large open space. The V-shaped trusses emphasize the span of the station and in the western arcade, modern vaulting at the eastern end melts and mirrors the shape of the original. It also provides welcome new shops and facilities and serves as a pedestrian link between the railway station and the London Underground. This is a transformative and very welcome change from the confusing and dilapidated station that it once was (just watch Dirk Bogarde's film *Password is Courage* and you get a feel for what it was like). It's no wonder that it won the 2019 RIBA London Building of the Year.

There are some other attractive design touches. Go to the Tooley Street entrance and as you look above the glass-and-steel canopy you will see an intricate pattern of bricks emerging from the facade in a wonderful modern interpretation of the beautiful Victorian brickwork we are more used to seeing. Also outside, close to the base of The Shard building, is a new artwork, a 57-m- (187-ft-) long piece made from 250,000 individual glass mosaic pieces in a wonderful array of twenty-eight colours. It is by the artist Adam Nathaniel Thurman and looks like a more colourful and busier version of Eduardo Paolozzi's (1924–2005) mosaics for Tottenham Court Road Underground Station. Finally, *Me.Here.Now.* by the artist Mark Titchner (b.1973) provides enveloping polished steel canopies on the ceiling of one of the station's stock-brick arched pedestrian walkways. Composed of a series of three metal umbrella-like structures between 4.5–6.5m (14¾–16¼ft) across, it creates patterns and shadows on the brick arches and is apparently about travel and self-reflection.

All this however is a world away from an engraving from the mid-nineteenth century entitled *South Eastern Railway Station, London Bridge.* It is a bustling scene with stuccoed Georgian architecture, horse-drawn carriages and what looks like a metal gateway emblazoned with the name of locations such as Brighton, Reigate, Croydon and Epsom.

In some ways, London Bridge had similar challenges and complications as our first station Victoria. The very first station was opened at Tooley Street in 1836 by the London and Greenwich Railway, who leased its railway line and station to other railway companies. This meant partnerships with the London & Croydon Railway and the London & Brighton and South Eastern Railway. Similar to Victoria, different companies established and operated in different parts of the station, so even though eventually a joint station was built, there was a dividing wall physically separating the north side from the south.

The railway companies eventually merged and in 1923 the Southern Railway started work on making a unified station by taking down the dividing wall and linking the two sides with a footbridge. It's no wonder that the station was confusing, as it was never really designed in a holistic way.

The changed station that we see today started as a concept in 2013 and owed its existence to Thameslink. Its design, the signage and accessibility are now a benchmark for how stations ought to be and has acted as a catalyst for change in the adjoining urban areas. Not only is there a new station, but it also has musical accompaniment. While a handful of London railway stations might have a piano, London Bridge has its own organ. Henry, to give the instrument its proper name, is a Victorian pipe organ built in 1880 and was moved to its current location to be used by the public in 2022 as part of the 'pipe up for pipe organs' charity project, which had rescued the organ after the church that had housed it closed down. Most famously, the organist Anna Lockwood gave a performance of 'God Save the King' accompanied by station security guards in September 2022.

8–9

LONDON
AND
SOUTH WESTERN
RAILWAY

JOURNEY

13

# FROM SUBURBAN LINES TO COASTAL TRACKS

## WATERLOO *to* SWANAGE

WATERLOO

SURBITON

BOURNEMOUTH WEST JUNCTION BOX

BOURNEMOUTH

SWANAGE RAILWAY

Journeying along this railway route offers a tapestry of stories and architecture, from Waterloo, where James Robb Scott's Victory Arch stands as a poignant memorial to the railwaymen lost in the Great War, its bronze plaques quietly bearing witness, to Surbiton which exudes the optimistic modernism of Art Deco, a symbol of a commuter age embracing the future. At Bournemouth, Queen Anne industrialism asserts itself, while the Swanage Railway recalls an age of steam, volunteer passion bringing it back to life amidst the craggy limestone of Purbeck. It's a journey shaped as much by the architects as by the landscapes, all echoing Britain's enduring relationship with its railways.

21
22
23
24
23
22

## WATERLOO

Memorably, the second verse of the Kinks' 1967 song 'Waterloo Sunset' has Terry meeting Julie at the station every Friday night. Although centred round Waterloo Bridge, very few railway stations are immortalized in popular song like Waterloo (there is Pet Shop Boys' 'King's Cross', but it's not quite as positive).

I always wonder where Terry met Julie. In terms of meeting places, the Waterloo Station clock is as iconic as the Glasgow Station clock in Journey 11 and had a sticker on the station floor stating: 'meet me under the clock.' The clock itself was made by Gents of Leicester and is believed to date back to the 1920s. Unusually for the time, it also has a 24-hour inner dial. In terms of scale, it is smaller than the one in Glasgow, with each of its four dials, 1.68m (5ft 6in) in diameter. It was restored in 2010 by specialist clockmaker Smith of Derby, the parent company of J. B. Joyce & Co, which made the clock in Holyhead in Journey 7.

The clock is regularly depicted in station posters of Waterloo Station, one of the best known being the series of two illustrations by artist Helen McKie (1889–1957) showing Waterloo Station at wartime and during peace, which appears on jigsaws even today. She had a prolific career as an illustrator for many magazines including *Bystander*, *Graphic*, *Sphere*, *Autocar* and *Queen*. In the Second World War, she was commissioned to sketch naval images for Lord Lloyd, paint a picture of 'The Upper War Room' for presentation to Sir Winston Churchill and worked for Southern Railway.

*(above) Concourse at Waterloo Station with Guardsmen on their way to practise for the Coronation*

*(opposite) The Grimshaw extension to Waterloo Station*

*'My brother went to church at the Foundling Hospital in the morning, still in ignorance of what had happened on the previous night. There he heard allusions made to the invasion, and a special prayer for peace. Coming out, he bought a REFEREE. He became alarmed at the news in this, and went again to Waterloo station to find out if communication were restored.'*

H.G. Wells, *The War of the Worlds*

**JAMES ROBB SCOTT**
(1882–1965)

As I have researched these journeys and come across multitudes of architects and engineers, I have realized that many of them are not as well-known as they deserve to be. A contemporary of Charles Holden, known for his modernist designs on the Underground system, Scott is definitely one of these and deserves to be better remembered.

James Robb Scott was a Scottish architect, born in the Gorbals in Glasgow, son of Andrew Robb Scott (1850–1914 – see Journey 10), who became the chief architect of the Southern Railway, designing many seminal stations including the art-deco masterpiece, Surbiton, as well as the offices of Waterloo Station and the Victory Arch, the only listed part of the station.

He joined the London & Southwestern Railway in 1906 (according to their employment records), employed initially as a draughtsman at the rate of £3 6s 0d per week. He must have been very well regarded as he was promoted to chief architectural assistant in the period of the reconstruction of Waterloo Station between 1909 and 1923.

He designed some of the most striking modernist masterpieces along the Southern Railway route, working with Edwin Maxwell Fry on Ramsgate (1926), which we visited in Journey 12, and then on his own at Malden Manor and Tolworth, with their sleek, crisp, flowing lines, over a rendered facade, both built in 1938 before the onset of war. He was also innovative in his use of concrete, as shown in the platform canopies of the lesser-known Chessington North Station (1939). He also embraced the brick art-deco Metroland aesthetic of the time, adding his own flourish and architectural masterpieces such as Bishopstone (1938), with its octagonal booking hall and geometric sky lights, and Horsham (1938), with fabulous brick detailing and swooping curves.

*Victory Arch at Waterloo Station*

Other pieces of art actually in the station include Peter Laszlo Peri's (1899–1967) Festival of Britain sculpture *The Sunbathers*. This was a lost piece of art that was found by a couple in the garden of the Clarendon Hotel in Blackheath, London after a campaign by Historic England. Its restoration was crowdfunded and it is now on show in Waterloo.

As the only railway station that features prominently in an alien attack, Waterloo was featured as the place where troops left to go and fight the Martians in Surrey in *The War of the Worlds*, as well as the location for getting information about was happening elsewhere in country during the invasion.

On to the rest of the station, which was originally opened in 1848 and named Waterloo Bridge; it was designed by Sir William Tite (also responsible for Carlisle – Journey 9) by the London and South Western Railway. Intriguingly, the original terminus was Nine Elms but it was replaced by Waterloo, as this was geographically closer to the West End. However, it was never meant to be a terminus and the line was due to go through to the City of London. The station was rebuilt in the early twentieth century, re-opening in 1922, and included the Victory Arch over the main entrance (built 1919–22), which commemorated the First World War. Grade II listed, the Victory Arch and adjoining facade was designed by James Robb Scott with engineers J. W. Jacomb-Hood (1859-1914) and Alfred Weeks Szlumper (1858–1934) responsible for the roof and platforms.

Quite harshly, the Historic England listing states, 'The rest of the station is not of special architectural or historic interest'. I would personally disagree. Beyond the long Scott facade designed in phases, there are moments of architectural interest: the concourse and platform glazed roofs; the station clock that I've already mentioned; the Grimshaw extension for Eurostar; and smaller details such as the stained-glass window in the Network Rail offices.

*(opposite) Surbiton Station*

*(below) Stained glass window in Waterloo Station*

Going back to Terry and Julie and their Waterloo sunset, to get out on to the bridge in the sixties, it's very likely they would have left via Scott's Victory Arch. Perhaps they would have paused at the head of the impressive flight of steps, under the triumphal arch, looked at the bronze plaques or the 1918 sculpture dedicated to peace; before going to view their sunset away from the crowds.

The bronze plaques under the arch bear the names of 585 London and South Western Railway employees who lost their lives in the First World War. The two sculptural groups are by Charles Whiffen (1867–1929), one dedicated to Bellona (dated 1914) and the other to peace, beneath the names of battlefields that are arrayed around a glazed arch set with a clock in a sunburst, and overseen on the roof by Britannia. What is particularly special is that London and South Western Railway staff were consulted about the design; you can almost imagine them looking and commenting on early versions of the watercolour drawing signed by Scott, which is held in the Network Rail archive.

### SURBITON

Four stops on and we are at another of James Robb Scott's stations. Widely recognized as an art-deco masterpiece, Surbiton Station is in the heart of London's commuterland. Interestingly, the London & Southampton Railway never meant to have Surbiton as a station; their preferred route was through Kingston, but Kingston, fearing for its coaching trade, refused to have a station built there.

The first station at Surbiton was completed in 1867, but it was totally rebuilt in 1937 to the design we see today. Grade II listed, it is a symphony in reinforced concrete that celebrates the future rather than the past of the railways. Happily, the original wood and bronze doors remain intact, with their triple bronze bars in front of long narrow panes

*(below) Bournemouth West Junction signal box*

*(opposite) Bournemouth Station as seen from Platform 3*

of glass, along with the sans serif typeface on the canopy announcing the name of the station, as well as the marble-lined booking hall.

Sadly, not all of the station has fared as well. The 1984 wall mural *Passengers* by Graeme Willson (1951–2018) and the one on the ceiling by Sue Ridge were pulled down during some work at the station and never returned. More positively though, in 2023, ten William Blake Mosaics, which form part of a set of seventy mosaics created by Southbank Mosaics to commemorate Blake's time in Lambeth between 1790 and 1800, were installed in Surbiton Station and form part of the Surbiton Art Trail.

Surbiton Station isn't just known for its architecture. It also appears in Agatha Christie's Poirot *The Adventure of the Clapham Cook*, which was the first episode of the 1989 ITV series and, more recently, in the movie, *Harry Potter and the Half-Blood Prince*. Surbiton was used for the opening scenes where Harry is in a café reading the *Daily Prophet* about the Death Eater attack in London. The location is now a Caffè Nero/waiting room.

### BOURNEMOUTH WEST JUNCTION BOX

Before we arrive at Bournemouth, we will stop briefly at the West Junction Box, which until its closure in 2009 would have been an important part of making our journey to the seaside town possible.

The West Junction Box opened in 1882 to control the corner of a triangular junction just created connecting Bournemouth West Station with the London and South Western Railway's main line through Bournemouth Central. Constructed of brick with a timber superstructure under a Welsh slate roof, it is of a type 3a design (railways had different designs of signal boxes, depending on location and traffic). Set above the ground-floor front

windows is a name board, reading 'West Junction' in a sans serif font. At first floor level, both the front and side elevations are fully glazed except for the entrance in the east end wall. It is listed Grade II, as it is one of the few rare remaining examples of a signal box type that has remained on the previous L&SWR and retains all its operating equipment, including its original mechanical twenty-four-lever Steven's frame.

Approximately 160 signal boxes are listed across the country, but as the last remaining ones close down and are replaced with digital signalling in regional operating centres, it becomes particularly important to document operations and people associated with these signal boxes. The Friends of the National Railway Museum have coordinated with various other bodies to record railway signalling as it stood in the middle of the second decade of the twenty-first century and have created the Film Archive of Railway Signalling & People (FARSAP).

Historic England has also produced two documents that chronicle the history of the signal box, one in 2012 by John Minnis and the other dated 2016 which is a comprehensive history of signal boxes. Both include the West Junction box.

### BOURNEMOUTH

Bournemouth Railway Station was known previously as Bournemouth East (1885–99) and then Bournemouth Central (1899–1967).

The station was designed by William Jacomb (1832–87), chief engineer of the L&SWR, and built in 1885. The station is substantial and constructed in red brick. The Grade II listing narrative describes it 'the most elaborate of the stations designed in the Queen Anne style'. I would add that it is a more industrial version of the Queen Anne aesthetic. It has a wonderfully detailed stucco entrance below a glazed porte-cochère. It is pedimented and has

*Swanage Station*

detailed leaf motif sculpted either side with the stylized '1885' written just above. The glazed roof, which is one the most attractive parts of the station, is supported on cross girders similar to those of Carlisle by Sir William Tite (1847) and Stoke-on-Trent by Henry Arthur Hunt (1848).

By 1967, third rail electrification had reached Bournemouth. As a celebration, British Transport Films created a short ten-minute infomercial about the benefits compared with the old steam locomotives. The film follows different groups of people from Waterloo to Bournemouth. It's worth seeing for wonderful historic shots of both Waterloo and Bournemouth stations, although the now slightly dated scene that stays with me is not the silver service that the main character gets for his breakfast on the train, or the slightly shifty way he occasionally looks at the other passengers, but the part where a 'businessman' rests his cigarette vertically on the small table beside him and the voiceover says that it 'gives cigarettes a better ride too'. Definitely another era!

## THE HERITAGE RAILWAY ASSOCIATION

The Heritage Railway Association (HRA) is the UK trade body representing heritage railways and associated entities.

The HRA says its membership operates:
- 173 working railways
- 9 operational tramways
- 8 cliff railways
- 24 museums and steam centres

Using:
- 901km (560 miles) of track
- 460 stations
- 800 steam locomotives
- 1,000 diesel locomotives
- 6,000 carriages and wagons

This is supported by:
- 100 societies, funding groups and locomotive and carriage owning trusts
- 22,000 volunteers
- 4,000 paid employees

To put this into context, as of 2023 there were 2,578 stations on the mainline railway and 15,845km (9,846 miles) of track.

## SWANAGE RAILWAY

Construction on the Swanage Railway began in May 1883, and the line opened in May 1885. It was amalgamated with the larger London and South Western Railway in 1886 as a terminus station. The railway was built under the supervision of consulting civil engineer W. R. Galbraith (Journey 11). A civil engineer employed by London and South Western Railway as a consulting engineer for over forty years, he oversaw the design and construction of nearly all that company's new lines between 1862 and 1907, when he retired. He also worked for other railway lines, most notably the London Underground on the Baker Street & Waterloo Railway, which became what we now know today as the Bakerloo Line.

In 1972 passenger service was withdrawn as the line became unprofitable and, in 1974, Swanage Station was sold to the local council. A year later, in 1975, the council gave Swanage Railway a lease for Swanage Station. Volunteers began to repair the station and relay the track, although progress was slow as the work was by hand and was heavy

and slow. Finally, in 1979, the railway operated its first passenger train. In 1992 the line reached Corfe Castle and eventually, in 1995, the trains reached Norden. Now in full operation on the Isle of Purbeck, it runs from Norden to Swanage through Corfe Castle, with full-size steam and diesel passenger trains along 9km (5½ miles) of line.

The Swanage Railway Museum based in Corfe Castle tells the story of the railway and is slightly set back from the main station building on the opposite side to the signal box.

Swanage Station itself is Grade II listed and is similar in architectural style to the rest of the stations along the route. It a long rectangular building, made of limestone with a low pitch, slate roof and a green flat wooden canopy with the station name written across. It also played a part as scenes set at Woking Station in the Christopher Nolan film *Dunkirk*. The station was partially closed and transformed with period props, and many locals were cast as extras.

*(opposite) Corfe Castle view from West Street*

*(above) Corfe Castle Signal Box*

JOURNEY

14

# THE LIMESTONE ROUTE

## KING'S CROSS *to* LINCOLN

KING'S CROSS

DIGSWELL VIADUCT

CAMBRIDGE

STAMFORD

LINCOLN ST MARKS (LOST STATION)

LINCOLN

Starting at King's Cross, a monument to Victorian innovation, we venture to the Digswell Viaduct, its arches soaring over pastoral landscapes – a tribute to Cubitt's engineering genius. Cambridge, with its elegant colonnades, reflects the city's academic gravitas and at Stamford, Jacobean-style limestone blends seamlessly with local heritage. The journey concludes in Lincoln, where classical and Gothic designs converge, crowned by Boole's legacy – a pioneer whose mathematical innovations shaped railway signalling and modern computing.

*King's Cross Station facade*

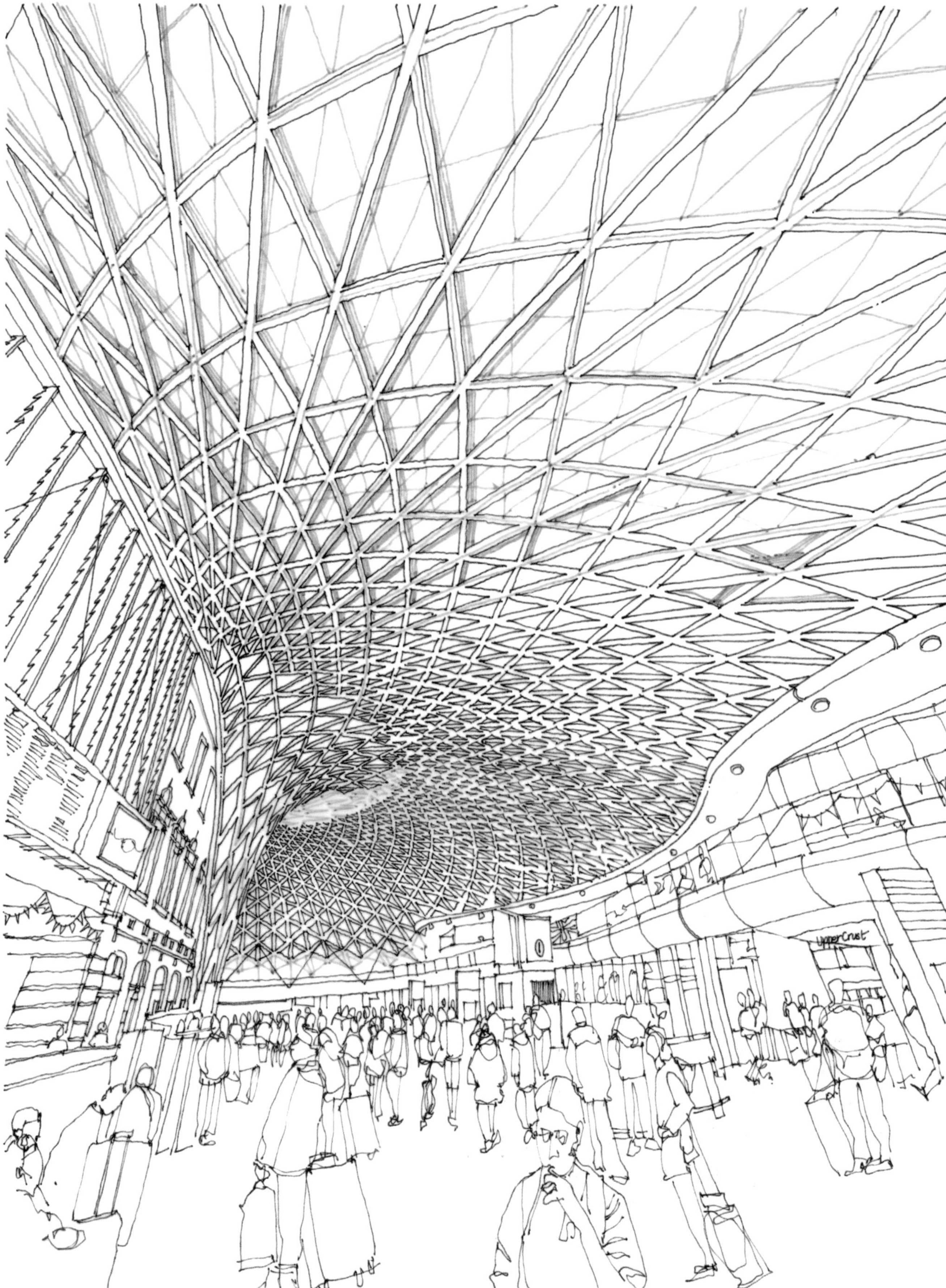
Upper Crust

## KING'S CROSS

The current King's Cross Station was built in 1851–52 as the London terminus of the Great Northern Railway (GNR), and was the fifth London terminal to be constructed. George Turnbull (1809–89), as resident engineer for the Great Northern Railway, made initial plans for the construction in December 1848. The detailed design for King's Cross was made by William Cubitt (1785–1861), who had been consulting engineer to Great Northern and engineer-in-chief to the South Eastern Railway, the chief engineer for Crystal Palace and eventually became Lord Mayor of London. Joseph Cubitt (1811–72), his son, was also responsible for the engineering works and, keeping it in the family, so was his brother Lewis Cubitt (1799–1883), who designed many of the developments that were planned by their other brother, Thomas Cubitt (1788–1855). Lewis also designed the Great Northern Hotel next door to King's Cross, the Granary building in King's Cross Central (now home to Central St Martin's) and London Bridge Station. There is a blue plaque to him located at the south-west corner of King's Cross Station close to one of the entrances to the London Underground station, naming him as the station's architect. King's Cross was listed Grade I in 1954.

The design of King's Cross included train-shed roofs of laminated wood, inspired by work William Cubitt had done on Crystal Palace; unfortunately these degraded and needed to be replaced by the iron ribs in the station today. The facades in yellow stock brick are unchanged, with two glazed semicircular openings framed in arches, recalling the shape of the train sheds behind them. At each side are central and flanking towers.

The central tower contains clock faces. These were designed by Edward Dent and had previously won a Council Medal for strength, accuracy and lower cost at the Great Exhibition of 1851 (where they were featured on the British Avenue) before being installed at the station. Interestingly, the three bells attached to the clock (bass, tenor and treble) had also been at the Great Exhibition, and received a medal.

The station, the biggest in England at the time, opened on 14 October 1852, but it only had one arrival and one departure platform, so it is not surprising that the station needed to be regularly expanded and have platforms added. A number of famous trains have been associated with King's Cross, including Sir Nigel Gresley's *Flying Scotsman* service to Edinburgh, and the streamlined A4 Pacific steam locomotives, including the most famous of the class, the *Mallard*.

Of course railways are as much about people as the trains and infrastructure. Wilston Samuel Jackson (1927–2018) became Britain's first Black train driver in 1962, and went on to drive famous trains and locomotives such as the *Mallard*, *Flying Scotsman* and *The Elizabethan*. Fittingly, there is a plaque to him at King's Cross Station. There is a similar plaque at Euston Station to honour Asquith Xavier, the first Black train guard at the station.

Finally, just as the original station developments and expansions ripped apart the urban fabric of London around King's Cross, the regeneration of the railway lands by Argent as master developer, Porphyrios Associates and Allies Morrison as the master planners and John McAslan + Partners for the redevelopment of King's Cross Station, have been part of a piece of city rebuilding that has used transport as a catalyst and restitched the city back together again. Starting from the late nineties, historic buildings and structures at King's Cross have been restored, reused and sometimes even relocated, such as the listed Gasholder No. 8 and the Gasholder Triplets, moved to house an urban park and a new residential development.

It has been an excellent example of regeneration, rejuvenating a part of the city that had become run down and dangerous, with both St Pancras and King's Cross acting as the anchors. The modernization and extension of King's Cross Station itself with its 'structurally dramatic wave-form roof' over the new concourse, designed by McAslan and Arups, has ensured the station will be fit for the future.

## DIGSWELL VIADUCT

Just outside Welwyn Garden City and to the south of Welwyn North Station, is the Digswell Viaduct (also known as the Welwyn Viaduct), which today carries the East Coast Mainline over the River Mimram. It was built between 1848–50,

*The McAslan/Arup new extension to King's Cross Station*

**SIR NIGEL GRESLEY**
(1876–1941)

There is an unassuming brown upholstered chair with a curved back and a small brass plaque on its back in the National Railway Museum warehouse. If you didn't know who it belonged to, you might not give it a second look or read the small print on the plaque. If you did, you would see, 'This chair was used by Sir Nigel Gresley. Chief Mechanical Engineer. LNER 1923–1941'. It belonged to one of Britain's best locomotive engineers.

Ask an average person (not a railway aficionado!) to name the most famous train they have heard of, and the chances are that a number would name the (A3) *Flying Scotsman* or the *Mallard*, the fastest steam locomotive in the world, which reached the speed of 203km/h (126mph) on 3 July 1938, and were both designed by Gresley.

Gresley began his engineering apprenticeship in 1893 under Francis Webb at the Crewe locomotive works (Journey 9) of the London North Western Railway. Just over ten years later, in 1905, he became the carriage and wagon superintendent to the Great Northern Railway. Gresley succeeded Henry Ivatt as locomotive engineer there, and in 1923 he became chief mechanical engineer of the London and North Eastern Railway, following the merger that created the four major railway companies. It was the London and North Eastern Railway that introduced locomotives such as the *Mallard* and the famous services such as the *Flying Scotsman*.

Gresley's innovations included use of alloy steels, forged pistons and rods, and small cylinders to keep the weight of his locomotives down, streamlining, high-pressure water tube boilers and articulated carriages to save weight, a feature still used in the Eurostar and TGV trains. In the Science Museum there is an intricate, detailed drawing signed by Gresley of an A1 class 4-6-2 three-cylinder express passenger engine (otherwise known as the *Flying Scotsman* locomotive) that shows the beauty of the mechanics.

At our first stop on this journey, there is a statue of Gresley. It was unveiled in King's Cross on 5 April 2016 to commemorate the 75th anniversary of his death, and cast by sculptor Hazel Reeves.

*'Without knowing it perhaps we all owe much of the speed and comfort of our travelling to his genius.'*

*Manchester Evening News* on Sir Nigel Gresley – Monday, 7 April 1941

*Statue of Sir Nigel Gresley at King's Cross by sculptor Hazel Reeves*

*Looking up at Digswell Viaduct*

designed by William Cubitt and his son Joseph. Thomas Brassey (1805–70) was the contractor, a man of whom it was said that he had built about one-third of the railways in Britain (including the Liverpool to Manchester Railway in Journey 2), or one-twentieth of all railway track in the world.

The viaduct was opened on 6 August 1850 by Queen Victoria, or so the story goes. The urban myth carries on that Queen Victoria was terrified of the 30-m (100-ft) height of the structure and so she never went across the viaduct, instead preferring to transfer on to a horse-drawn carriage and travel the length on the ground. However it has been proven via her published journals that she was over 150km (100 miles) away at Osborne House, her home on the Isle of Wight. The *Sun* newspaper from that very day has a report on the opening of the viaduct and it appears that this was actually undertaken by 'Mr Beckett Denison MP (the chairman of the Great Northern Railway), supported by Mr Packe, the deputy-chairman' (facts confirmed by a report from the *Hertford and Mercury Reformer* on 10 August 1850). The reporter goes on to write, 'This viaduct was much admired by all parties; the engineering skill displayed in its construction eliciting general and warm commendations.'

The viaduct itself is of forty arches and a Grade II* listed structure. It is approximately 475m (1,560ft) long with a span of 9m (30ft). It was the longest and tallest viaduct on the Great Northern Railway's route. Constructed of red brick fired from clay quarried on site during construction, it needed restoration in the 1930s, when the viaduct's deteriorating brickwork was encased in the blue engineering brick seen today.

## CAMBRIDGE

Plans to have a station at Cambridge go back to 1822, when the first survey for the line was made. However, the station's

*Exterior of Cambridge Station, with some of the thirty-two Cambridge College roundels*

first brick wasn't laid until 10 April 1845. It – and the new line between Cambridge and Bishop's Stortford – opened just three months later on 29 July, initially serving Bishopsgate Station in London via Stratford and Bishop's Stortford. The line between Cambridge and Norwich opened a day later.

The *Cambridge General Advertiser* of 30 July 1845 starts by stating:

*'The revolutions effected throughout the country by the introduction of the "way of iron" superseding the old high road have not until now been brought immediately before the eyes of the quiet dwellers in Cambridge. They have heard of them from the lips of others and have witnessed perhaps in other places the magic changes performed by the potent enchanter Steam – The barren wilderness has becom e a great city and the desolate places have been to blossom as the rose.'*

The article also contains illustrations of the station with its fifteen tall arches, built of white gault brick, all of which, at the time, were open like a colonnade with lamps hanging from the apex of the arches. The station's thrity-two roundels represent the coats of arms of Cambridge University's colleges, dating back to the opening of the station in 1845 and were recently painstakingly restored.

There is some discussion as to the main architect of the station. The listing mentions Sancton Wood (1814–86) who was trained in classical architecture by his uncle, the famous architect Robert Smirke (1780–1867), who went on to have a successful career in railway architecture in Britain and Ireland, although other sources also credit the design to architect Francis Thompson who became particularly well known for his stations in the Midlands and railway town of Derby (Journey 11).

The station also has had its fair share of royal visitors. Two years after its opening, in 1847, Queen Victoria used Cambridge Station for the installation of Prince Albert as the Chancellor of Cambridge University and, nearly thirty years later, in 1873, it went from a real royal visit to a hoax one. It was reported that the Shah of Iran was due to come to Cambridge as part of his three-week state visit to Britain. Unfortunately, after the city and university dignitaries assembled in haste in front of the station to welcome him, it became apparent that the Shah was not coming at all.

Cambridge
Cambridge

## STAMFORD

Just over an hour later, we arrive at our next station, Stamford, which used to be known as Stamford Town to distinguish it from Stamford East, which was closed to passengers in 1957. It was built in 1848 for the Syston & Peterborough Railway, to the designs of Sancton Wood, who was also involved in designing Cambridge Station.

Built as a result of an Act allowing the Midland Railway Company to build the Syston to Peterborough Railway, the line was meant to follow the river through the town, but the Marquis of Exeter, who owned most of Stamford, insisted on a cut-and-cover tunnel so that the railway could not easily be seen and, more importantly, did not impinge on the views from his residence at Burghley House. It is therefore hardly surprising that Sancton Wood cited Burghley House as an important influence on his design, presumably to curry favour with an important stakeholder. In reality, it is much less decorated and utilitarian in appearance and even its massing tends to a more angular style than the rounded towers and numerous decorative chimney stacks that grace the skyline of Burghley.

That's not to say that Stamford Station does not have its own charms. It was upgraded to a Grade II* listing due to its exceptional architectural and historic interest. Constructed from local oolitic limestone and Collyweston slates, with steeply pitched roofs, octagonal chimney stacks and arrow slit windows, it is more Jacobean in appearance, with a wonderful iron-latticed footbridge across its two platforms and an almost unchanged nineteenth-century waiting room.

For over a quarter of a century, the former stationmaster's house also housed Robert Humm & Co, an incredibly friendly and helpful bookshop specializing in rare and out-of-print books about railways, other transport and industrial history, as well as a wide selection of new books on railways.

### LINCOLN ST MARKS (LOST STATION)

The official opening of Lincolnshire's first railway took place on 3 August 1846, although it is suggested by newspaper reports that only a wooden temporary station was ready for the opening of the line. Once permanently built, the station building was a single storey with seventeen bays designed in a neo-classical style with an Ionic portico and fluted columns and side pavilions with Doric pilasters. The building is Grade II listed.

As with Cambridge Station, there is some discussion as to the actual architect. It is attributed to William Adams Nicholson (1803–53), although John A. Davies (1796–1865) has also been suggested as the architect. Nicholson was a founding member of RIBA. He was prolific, and designed a number of workhouses, town halls, and in Lincoln, the County Prison in Lincoln Castle, the first Lincoln Corn Exchange and the Lincoln Stock Library (sadly demolished with a House of Fraser now occupying the site), as well as numerous churches, chapels and country houses. Davies trained under George Maddox (1760–1843), who was particularly well-known for his Greek revival style in central London. Most of Davies' buildings were also Greek revival in style, but sadly few of them survive.

In 1848, two years after Lincoln St Marks began operating, Lincoln acquired a second station, Lincoln Central. Over a century later, St Marks was slated for closure as part of the Beeching cuts, but initially got a reprieve. It was eventually closed in 1985, to avoid the unnecessary operation of two stations, and services were diverted to Lincoln Central.

*(opposite) Exterior, Stamford Station*

*(above) Exterior of Lincoln St Marks – its former station is now used for retail*

Sections of the station buildings survive today as part of a main shopping street. The grand portico is now a shop as opposed to a station entrance, and a mock signal box has been built in the car park, where an original sign from the station has been affixed.

## LINCOLN

Originally the lesser of the two Lincoln stations, the end of this journey, initially named Lincoln Central, was completed two years after Lincoln St Marks. Also Grade II listed, it is thought to be the work of John Henry Taylor (1791–1867) (although the Historic England listing also questions whether it might be Joseph Cubitt) for the Great Northern Railway. It is built in yellow brick with steeply pitched slate roofs and a castellated pyramidal tower overlooking the whole station, although from some angles it is reminiscent of an educational establishment rather than a railway station. The frontage is particularly grand beneath a four-bay glazed canopy with two central Gothic arched doors in the middle.

What is also particularly interesting is the recent sculpture of George Boole in front of the station. It is funded by the Heslam Trust (which has been purchasing, or contributing to the purchase of art for the citizens of Lincoln since 1963) and made by sculptor Antony Dufort (b.1948). Boole, the father of Boolean logic and algebra, was born in Lincoln in 1815. It is his work that paved the way for the computer that we now take for granted and which allows us to do internet searches. He also taught both girls and boys at a time when education for women was not widely accepted. His work is very pertinent to our book – Boolean mathematic and logic is the basis for all railway signalling.

*(left) Stonework detail inside Lincoln Station with the letters 'GNR'*

*(opposite) Outside Lincoln Station with statue of George Boole*

# COMING HOME

When I first had the idea of writing (and drawing!) this book, I was hopeful that by the time I reached this concluding chapter, I would be describing the journey into what would be, at least be on paper, a settled design for a new Euston Station and the home of a new highspeed rail.

However, life and complex programme management never go in straight lines and major infrastructure has a habit of not entirely going to plan, either. So, instead we start our final journey at Birmingham Curzon Street, metres away from where foundation works have just started for what will be Britain's first new intercity terminus since the nineteenth century and net zero in operation, while at the other end, designs continue to be worked through for Euston.

I want to linger here next to the surviving structure of the original Curzon Street or what used to be simply called Birmingham Station when it was first opened in 1838. The Grade I listed entrance building designed by Philip Hardwick (1792–1870) and built by Peto & Grissell (yes, who else? – see Journey 4), costing £26,000, was actually not part of the main train station but initially an office and then a kind of hotel with event spaces. If you squint a little at the building currently marooned in the middle of the HS2 work site, you can see the resemblance to the more famous Euston Arch, also designed by Hardwick. The two structures bookended the line.

*The Times* described building the building at the time as:

*'The general office in front of the station is of a magnificent character, and is intended for meetings of the directors and the offices of the secretary. The ground floor, when the building is completed, will be appropriated for the refreshments for passengers, under the direction of Mr Dee, of the Royal Hotel.'*

The word 'magnificent' here is important. People literally wanted the architecture of these buildings to reflect the significance of the railways,

*The original Curzon Street Station*

something that the new Curzon Street looks likely to do in its sweeping grid shell roof. Therefore, as part of this last journey, I want to reflect on our travels and the 100 or so stations that I have drawn and ask: what are the ingredients from the past 200 years that make a really good station?

But it can't just be about looks, or a sketch that looks great penned on a paper napkin by a starchitect but that then either doesn't quite have the functionality, is style over substance or turns its back on the city and the context it is placed within. Nor can it be part of the other extreme; fully functional but dull, and uninspired to an extent that makes you wonder if it was Marvin the Paranoid Android (the supercomputer from *The Hitchhiker's Guide to the Galaxy*) who designed it.

To avoid design by depressed artificial intelligence, I have tried to distil into seven ingredients what a station needs to be:

### A) CONNECTS THE CITY

The redevelopment of the lands behind St Pancras and King's Cross is an exemplar as well as a case study in patience and resilience. It shows what can be achieved with the right funding, foresight, an excellent group of architects

*Placemaking at King's Cross Central*

and designers and two major transport termini bringing connectivity, footfall and anchoring to nearly 30 hectares (around 75 acres) of previously semi-derelict railway land, transforming it into what is now a major new neighbourhood. It not only stitches back what was ripped apart by the arrival of the railways, but does it with panache, despite the number of physical constraints that it faced, including a plot of smallpox burials and a veritable graveyard of previous failed schemes. Today it boasts a new vibrant office quarter, shopping, restaurants, and the new campus for Central St Martins, all without losing the structures that make you think back to its railway heritage.

### B) IMPROVES THE PUBLIC REALM

Public realm that is poorly maintained or designed in such a way that the Great British weather batters you before you have managed to get to your train home is something sadly familiar to the regular rail traveller. Phase one of the council's wider public realm plan, Eastbourne is a welcome exception to this, and proves that spaces outside stations can be elegant, and simply designed with a modest budget that links to the surrounding streets in an attractive and safe way. This is done through the creation of a shared surface and partial pedestrianisation of the area around the station, a harmonious space targeted for the traveller, rather than a space for the pedestrian to play a game of chicken trying to dodge cars and buses whilst trying to get their train.

### C) SENSE OF ARRIVAL AND GRANDEUR

You've made it into the station. Does it lift your spirits or make you dread your commute? What is the first thing you see? Banks of ticket machines? Low fake ceilings? Or an expanse of space that celebrates travel?

Liverpool Lime Street frames the city. Stepping out, with the worst of the post-war development gone, you see St George's Hall, the National Museum of Liverpool and the Walker Art Gallery before you, while the graceful curve of the long, glass, nineteenth-century roof positively welcomes you into the station. Further north, Edinburgh Waverley is the antithesis to the sight of phalanxes of ticket machines. The 35-m- (115-ft-) wide glass, leaded dome over the Booking Hall is probably one the most impressive places to pay for your onward journey.

### D) BECOMES AN INTEGRATOR FOR OTHER PUBLIC TRANSPORT & IS EASILY ACCESSIBLE

How easy is it to go from one part of the transport system to another? Will you miss your connection by the time you've gone to a different train service, or is it as easy as just walking gracefully across to another platform? Is the signage clear? Or is it a confused mixed of arrows with a strange font that points you in directions that require you to go through brick walls (fine if you are Harry or Hermione) or take flight? It doesn't matter how exquisitely designed your station is if it fails at the first hurdle of actually being able to get on your train.

While our train network has still some way to go to becoming truly accessible to all users, new and rebuilt stations with the aid of modern building standards are slowly making a change.

The new design for London Bridge Station, almost ten years in the making from contract to operation, solved the issues of accessibility, while also creating a vastly better interchange between the different train services as well as with the London Underground, out of what had been a historical mess in terms of levels and exits. The station has step-free access to and between all platforms at all times trains are running, via level access and lifts, while all entrances to the station also have step-free access. The architects Grimshaws describe it as using, 'the structural gestures, such as the upward arc of the ribbons, voids and rooflights, to guide people naturally to the platforms'.

In addition, there are hundreds of custom-made signs, all designed to meet Network Rail standards. Requirements ranged from significant architectural structures, like the directional signs suspended from the terminal roof, to more traditional signage such as the station's door signage, including 3,000 plaques, which just goes to show that less is not more where navigation is concerned.

*The grandeur of Liverpool Lime Street Station*

NERO
NERO

*Newcastle Castle as seen through the railway lines*

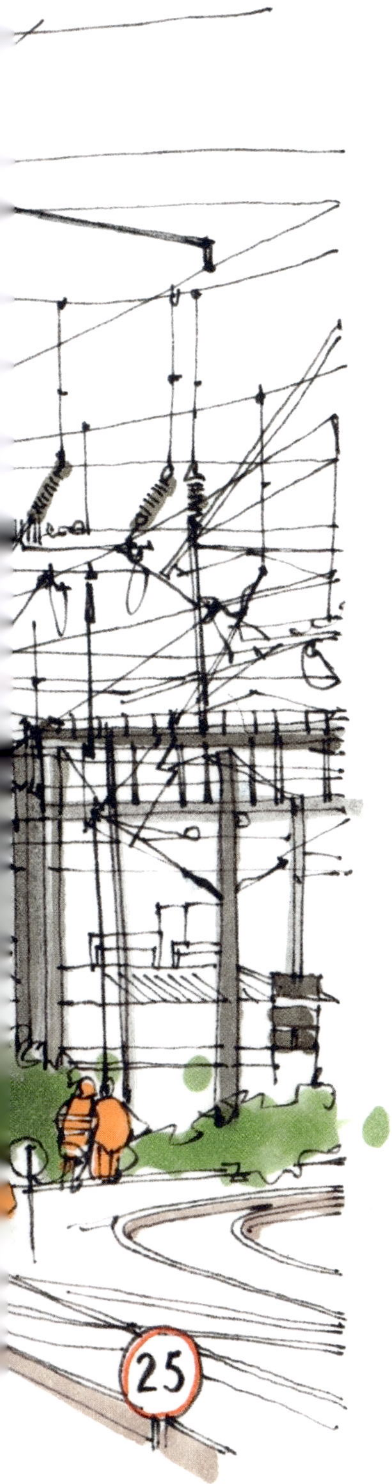


### E) GOOD AMENITIES

The range of facilities needed in stations depends on their scale and the numbers of passengers who they serve. There are the basics – clean and sufficient numbers of toilets, for example, and waiting rooms that protect from the elements – but these are the fundamentals. Sure, shops are important but Pitlochry's station bookshop, King's Lynn's Country Line Cafe and Paddington's first-class waiting room with its royal crests and its brass band, are what make stations memorable and special.

### F) REFLECTS THE HERITAGE

Whether it's coats of arms of a railway company that stopped operating over a century ago, wrought-iron designs at the tops of columns such as those in Great Malvern, York or Preston, or even the beautifully ornate gates of Glasgow Central, each of these details tells us about the past, the history of the railways and the place. It's not just about architectural embellishments, either. The sculptures in our stations, of Sir Nigel Gresley in King's Cross, Larkin in Hull, Boole in Lincoln or Bressie Braddock in Liverpool, tell us about the people and the lives the railways have touched. More substantially, Darlington has a whole series of panels describing the history of the first railway journey from Darlington to Stockton (Journey 1) and, not to be outdone, Newcastle Keep is just east of the East Coast Main Line going into Newcastle Central reminding us of a pre-industrial past.

Without these parts of history, it's like being in a glorified shed devoid of context and understanding, almost like a better built version of a motorway service station or some anonymous hotel lounge stuck in some in-between space purgatory, identifying with everywhere but of nowhere in particular. These don't need to be (and ideally shouldn't be) artefacts or pastiche, but the personality, history and the story of a place should be reflected in all our buildings.

### G) BEAUTY IN THE DETAIL

Finally, it's just as much about the small things as the larger context. It is the detail, the fixtures and fitting, the way structures are built and their quality that will ensure whether there is a lasting legacy or a structure that within merely two decades will need to be pulled down and built anew.

Worcester Shrub Hill's beautiful tiles in the waiting room are excellent examples of this. Paddington's ornate vent perforations are another and at the more modern end, the swooping structure in the concourse at King's Cross looks just as fresh as when it was opened. This includes the modest, uncelebrated details in a station like Coventry with its solid wood handrails, and glazed, well-lit spaces.

The final measurement of what makes a station building 'magnificent', as in the 1837 article from *The Times*, is more elusive. We should ask ourselves: will it be the kind of station that Sir Samuel Morton Peto would have wanted to bankroll and have his bust displayed in, as in Norwich? Would it stir the imagination enough for it to become a backdrop to a novel or get Sir John Betjeman excited enough to write about it and save it?

The stations we build today can inspire a new generation about the joys of rail travel. To do this they must be memorable, well-designed, contemporary yet linked to their heritage, human yet grand enough for a sense of arrival and, lastly, leave a legacy that will be remembered for the next bicentenary.

*Darlington Station and link to heritage through wrought-iron work and columns*

# INDEX

# ABOUT THE AUTHOR

Author and illustrator **Sherin Aminossehe** moved from Iran to the UK as a child, training as an architect, working across the world both in the government and private sector. Taught by her mother, she has been drawing since she could hold a pencil, and recently published the book *The Road Untravelled*, a Covid lockdown project for charity, wherein she took requests for drawings of longed-for destinations from London to Nepal, providing imaginary escape when no one could travel. From the Rocky Mountaineer to the Glacier Express and the Orient Express all the way to the 07:03 from King's Cross to Leeds or even Waterloo to Woking, Sherin loves train travel, ideally in a window seat with a sketchbook by her side.

# ACKNOWLEDGEMENTS

They always say books don't write themselves or in this case don't illustrate and write themselves either. There have been many people without whom this book would not have been finished.

My wonderful parents: **Mum, Minoo Razban** who taught me to draw with love and who I wish was here to see the book and my **Dad, Piroozan** who supported me through the whole process and watched me draw every evening on our Facetime calls; **Terence**, my lovely husband, who lived through every station and route and shared his love of railways with me, took a lot of the images that were used for reference, patiently listened to me agonise when things didn't go to plan and never said it was marginally mad to illustrate and write a book alongside a full-time job; **Lord Hendy of Richmond Hill** for giving his time so generously, sharing his knowledge of the railways and kindly writing the foreword for this book; **Network Rail** and the **Science Museum Group (especially the National Railway Museum)** and their archives for this book which allowed me to access places and information; **Kate Johnson**, my fabulous agent, who believed in me, shared her knowledge and gave me brilliant, wise advice when I had absolutely no clue how the publishing industry worked; everyone at **Quarto and Frances Lincoln** especially **Philip Cooper**, **Róisín Duffy** and **Laura Bulbeck** for their support, patience and magic; **Ocky Murray** for the beautiful book layout and bringing it all to life; **Philip Parker** for his incredible attention to detail and making sense of my text; **Dame Bernadette Kelly** at the **Department for Transport** who I initially talked about the book to; **Robert Humm & Co**, the amazing transport bookshop in Stamford for the box load of books you helped me find; **friends and colleagues at the Ministry of Defence** who politely and kindly listened to me talk about railways for the past year and half; and last but definitely not least to all those on social media, both friends and those who I only know virtually, who give me and my art so much support. I wouldn't have gone down this path without you.

Quarto

First published in 2025 by Frances Lincoln,
an imprint of The Quarto Group.
One Triptych Place, London, SE1 9SH,
United Kingdom
T (0)20 7700 9000
www.Quarto.com

EEA Representation, WTS Tax d.o.o., Žanova ulica 3,
4000 Kranj, Slovenia
www.wts-tax.si



A catalogue record for this book is available from the British Library.

ISBN 978-1-83600-483-7
Ebook ISBN 978-1-83600-484-4

10 9 8 7 6 5 4 3 2 1

Design by Ocky Murray

Publisher: Philip Cooper
Senior Editor: Laura Bulbeck
Editor: Róisín Duffy
Senior Designer: Isabel Eeles
Senior Production Manager: Alex Merrett

Printed in Guangdong, China TT062025

FSC www.fsc.org MIX Paper | Supporting responsible forestry FSC® C016973